As one of the world's longest establis
and best-known travel brands,
Thomas Cook are the experts in travel.

For more than 135 years our
guidebooks have unlocked the secrets
of destinations around the world,
sharing with travellers a wealth of
experience and a passion for travel.

**Rely on Thomas Cook as your
travelling companion on your next trip
and benefit from our unique heritage.**

Thomas Cook **traveller** guides

GREEK ISLANDS
Robin Gauldie

Thomas
Cook

Your travelling companion since 1873

Written and updated by Robin Gauldie

Published by Thomas Cook Publishing
A division of Thomas Cook Tour Operations Limited
Company registration no. 3772199 England
The Thomas Cook Business Park, Unit 9, Coningsby Road,
Peterborough PE3 8SB, United Kingdom
Email: books@thomascook.com, Tel: +44 (0) 1733 416477
www.thomascookpublishing.com

Produced by Cambridge Publishing Management Limited
Burr Elm Court, Main Street, Caldecote CB23 7NU
www.cambridgepm.co.uk

ISBN: 978-1-84848-542-6

© 2002, 2006, 2008, 2010 Thomas Cook Publishing
This fifth edition © 2012
Text © Thomas Cook Publishing
Maps © Thomas Cook Publishing/PCGraphics (UK) Limited

Series editor: Karen Beaulah
Production/DTP: Steven Collins

Printed and bound in India by Replika Press Pvt Ltd

Cover photography © Thomas Cook

Contents

Introduction

Variety is the spice of the Greek islands. Some visitors go in search of the ancient and medieval worlds of temples, castles and fortresses. Others seek peaceful harbour or hilltop villages and secluded coves. Millions more are simply looking for a good time in bustling holiday resorts with sandy beaches, friendly tavernas and discos. All of these are waiting to be discovered.

Typically, each island moves to its own rhythm. It has its own landscape, architecture and traditions which, though they may have basic shared characteristics, are also distinct.

Through the long summer months, Greek islanders spend most of their time outdoors, though they avoid the fierce middle-of-the-day temperatures by staying indoors and taking a siesta, which is why many places resemble ghost towns during the afternoon.

For visitors, there is no better way to while away the hot afternoons than to sit at a shady harbourside café with a glass of cold beer and a plate of octopus landed fresh that morning.

You can stay in the bright, newly built apartments and hotels of the popular resorts, seek out smaller pensions or village rooms in quiet hideaways, or find comfortably restored old homes, traditional shipowners' mansions or secluded luxury hotels.

The Aegean and Ionian seas offer some of the best yachting and windsurfing in Europe, in addition to waterskiing, parascending, diving and snorkelling from dozens of beaches.

Each group of islands has different attractions, and it pays to do some research before setting off on a journey of discovery. Island-hoppers have always favoured the Cyclades, which are close enough together that each 'hop' need take no more than a couple of hours. For a real sense of discovery, head for the larger islands of the Northeast Aegean, each of which has a distinctive history, geography and island culture. The Ionian island resorts offer the traditional package fortnight for families and groups of young singles, while also appealing to sailors. The Sporades, with some of the best beaches in Greece, also appeal to families with younger children. Crete, Greece's largest island, is a destination in its own right, with bustling resorts, peaceful villages, empty beaches, awesome mountains for walkers, historic towns and ancient ruins.

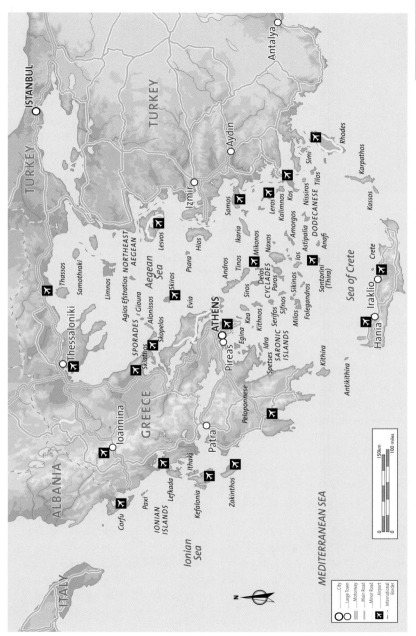

The land

Greece claims some 2,000 islands, islets, rocks and skerries, from Corfu, off the northwest coast, to Rhodes (and just beyond) in the southeast. Six of these, Corfu and its satellites, are in the Ionian Sea, a southern extension of the Adriatic. The rest clutter the Aegean Sea, with Crete separating them from the Eastern Mediterranean.

Climate

Each island has its own microclimate, influenced by the sea, prevailing winds and nearby land masses. Spring comes earliest to Crete, which also has the hottest summers. Rhodes has more hours of sunshine than any other island, while Corfu and the Ionian isles have slightly milder summers. The Cyclades are swept by the gale-force *meltemi*, which can blow for up to three days at a time in summer. Samos and the northeast Aegean islands, close to the Turkish coast, have late springs, influenced by the snowy heights of the Anatolian plateau. From late May to October, rain is rare.

Economy and population

About 1.3 million Greeks are islanders, living on 169 inhabited islands. Many of these have only a handful of natives, such as tiny Maratho. On the other hand, Crete is home to more than half a million.

Tourism is a big employer on many islands, but fishing and farming are still important. Quarrying for marble and pumice is also a contributor to several island economies.

Farming

Oranges, lemons, vines and, above all, olives grow abundantly on the more fertile islands. On smaller, drier isles, barley and wheat grow on terraces, and goats graze on higher ground. On the remoter islands, age-old implements and practices are only now being replaced by modern tools and methods.

Fishing

Island fishermen seek squid, sardines, mackerel, red mullet and other prizes. The Aegean has been fished intensively for millennia and catches are getting smaller, but demand is high and prices are increasing. Fish farms, raising sea bass and other species in floating cages, are increasingly big business.

Flora and fauna

Many of the islands are rewarding for snorkellers and birdwatchers, and a rich insect and reptile fauna includes species found nowhere else in Europe. Rare sea turtles nest on some island beaches (*see p42*). Wild flowers provide a blaze of spring colour.

Geology

Some islands are of porous limestone rock; others, like Samos, Samothraki or Ikaria in the Aegean Sea, are basalt outcrops. Santorini's unique landscapes are the result of millennia of volcanic activity, and Nissiros too has a slumbering volcanic crater. Marble is quarried on Paros and Thassos, and quarries on Milos and Santorini produce cement.

The sea

In ancient times, the sea linked the islands with the empires of Asia Minor and Egypt. In the 15th and 16th centuries, the sea spelt prosperity for some but, at the same time, peril for others from pirate raids. Greek island captains controlled the wealthy trade of the Ottoman empire, and during the War of Independence turned their guns on the Turks.

The sea also unites the scattered islands and provides a living for thousands of sailors and fishermen. Small sailing brigs (*trehandiri*) were the trade lifeline for many islands well into the 20th century, and every island has its quota of old salts from the Greek merchant navy.

The sea also provided an emigration route for islanders, most of them heading for the USA, Australia, Canada and South Africa. However, ties with the islands proved difficult to break, and many Greeks settled abroad still bring their families 'home' in the summer for a nostalgic visit.

The land

Deep natural harbours on many islands have helped shape Greece as a maritime nation

History

3000 BC	Seafaring Bronze Age trading culture develops in Cyclades.
2200–1700	Early Minoan civilisation in Crete develops into Minoan palace culture and trade empire.
1600	Mycenaean culture spreads to islands from Greek mainland.
***c.* 1470**	Explosion of volcano on Santorini. Collapse of Minoan civilisation.
1200	Waning of Mycenaean culture.
***c.* 1000**	Arrival of Dorian Greeks in Aegean islands.
800–600	City-state system emerges.
776	First Ancient Olympic Games in Olympia.
490	First Persian invasion. Athenian victory at Marathonas.
480	Second Persian invasion. Persian fleet destroyed at Salamis.
479	Persian defeats on mainland end Persian wars.
478	Athens dominates the islands as leader of Delian league.
431–404	Peloponnesian War between Sparta and Athens ends in Athenian defeat.
358–336	Rise of Macedonia.
336–323	Reign of Alexander the Great.

Mandraki harbour, Rhodes

323–196	Era of Macedonian kings.
215–146	Wars with Rome, culminating in Roman conquest.
1st century BC	Pompey clears pirates from Aegean islands.
AD 260–68	Gothic fleets raid islands.
330	Roman Emperor Constantine moves his capital to Byzantium (Istanbul), renaming it Constantinople and founding the Christian Byzantine empire.
600–900	Arab corsairs conquer Crete, sack Rhodes and raid Aegean islands.
960–61	Byzantine general Nikiforos Fokas recovers Crete.
1204	Frankish–Venetian Fourth Crusade sacks Constantinople. Venetians take Crete, the Ionian islands and Evia. Knights of St John take Rhodes, Kos and the Dodecanese. Cyclades come under rule of the Sanudo dukes of Naxos, vassals of the Frankish King of Athens. Genoa acquires northeast Aegean islands.
1354–1453	Turkish conquest of Byzantine empire ends in fall of Constantinople.
1499–1530	Turks conquer Venetian strongholds on mainland.
1522	Turks take Rhodes.
1566	Turks conquer Hios and Naxos.
1669	Turks capture Crete.
1797	Revolutionary France seizes Corfu and Ionian islands from Venice.
1814–64	British protectorate of Corfu and Ionian islands.
1821–30	War of Independence. Cyclades and Argo-Saronic islands, with parts of the mainland, form the new Republic of Greece.
1831	President Ioannis Capodistrias assassinated.
1833	Bavarian Prince Otto becomes King Otho I of the Hellenes (Greeks).

1864	Britain cedes Corfu and Ionian islands to Greece.
1866	Cretan revolt against Turkey fails.
1896	First Modern Olympic Games in Athens.
1912	First Balkan War. Greece annexes Hios. Italy seizes Rhodes and the Dodecanese from Turkey.
1913	Second Balkan War. Cretan revolt succeeds. Crete joins Greece after brief independence. Many Cretan Muslims migrate to Rhodes. Greece annexes Lesvos, Samos and Ikaria.
1917	World War I. Greece joins Britain, France and Italy.
1919	Encouraged by Britain and France, Greece lands troops at Smyrna (Izmir) in Turkey.
1920–23	War between Greece and Turkey ends in defeat for Greece. Around one million Greeks driven from Turkey.
1924–36	Political chaos. General Metaxas becomes dictator.
1940	Italian invasion defeated.
1941–4	German and Italian occupation of mainland and islands. Various resistance groups active, especially on Crete. British commando raids on Dodecanese islands.
1946–9	Civil war on mainland, with the USA and Britain supporting the Royalist right-wing government forces against the left.
1947	Rhodes and the Dodecanese join Greece.
1953	Earthquake affects Zakinthos and Santorini.
1967–74	Military junta led by Colonel George Papadopoulos rules Greece. King Constantine expelled. Referendum ends the monarchy.
1974	Collapse of the junta after the Turkish invasion of Cyprus. Restoration of democracy.
1981	Greece joins the European Community. Centre-left PASOK party led by Andreas Papandreou elected.

Rhodes became part of Greece in 1947

1989	PASOK defeated. Series of short-lived caretaker governments.
1990	Nea Dimokratia party elected under Konstantinos Mitsotakis.
1993 & '97	PASOK re-elected.
1997–8	Tension between Greece and Turkey over the ownership of uninhabited islands in the Northeast Aegean.
1998–9	Greek public opinion strongly opposed to NATO bombing of Serbia.
2001	PASOK re-elected. Greece enters the eurozone. Earthquake strikes Athens, affecting Skiros and other islands.
2004	Nea Dimokratia elected under Kostantinos Karamanlis.
	28th Summer Olympic Games in Athens.
2007	Corfu Old Town listed as a UNESCO World Heritage Site.
2008	Riots in Athens, Crete, Corfu and Kos.
2009	George Papandreou's PASOK party wins convincing election victory.
2010	Economic crisis leads to disturbances, strikes and demonstrations throughout Greece.
2011	Mass protests against sweeping austerity measures, including tax increases and cuts to wages in pensions, imposed as part of an international 'bail-out' for Greek economy. Papandreou resigns, to be replaced by a 'caretaker' coalition government headed by Loukas Papademos.
2012	Government continues austerity measures and attempts to speed up privatisation of public-sector companies. Strikes and protests continue.

Island dwellers

The Cyclades in the Bronze Age

The first metal-using civilisation in Greece flourished in the Cyclades around 3000 BC, leaving behind bronze tools and implements, and remarkably modern-looking carvings.

The Minoans

For five centuries, from around 2200 BC, the Minoan empire based on Crete was the greatest power in the Aegean, exacting tribute from mainland Greek princes and controlling colonies throughout the Cyclades.

The Mycenaeans and Dorians

As Minoan power waned, the warlike, bronze-using Mycenaeans (of Homer's sagas) expanded from the mainland into Crete and the Cyclades. Around 1100 BC they were followed by the first Greek-speaking, iron-using Dorian settlers.

The Classical era

In the city-state era, many of the islands possessed powerful navies and merchant fleets, and often vied with Athens for control of Greek seas. Several sided with Persia during the Persian Wars. At the height of its power, Athens controlled the Delian League of island states (those surrounding the sacred island of Delos), but many of the islands aligned themselves with Sparta against Athens during the Peloponnesian War.

Alexander and his heirs

With the rise of Macedonia, the islands came under the sway of Alexander and his successors, and the Ptolemies of Egypt used Santorini as a naval base.

The Romans

In 229 BC, Corfu and the Ionian group became the first Greek islands to fall to Rome. However, by the time Roman subjugation of Greece was completed, with the conquest of Athens in 86 BC, many of the Aegean islands had become pirate havens. The situation became so bad that in the 1st century BC the Roman general Pompey raised a fleet to clear the outlaws from the sea.

The Byzantine empire

The power of Constantinople waned in the 7th and 8th centuries AD and Arabs from Spain conquered Crete, sacked Rhodes and raided the Aegean islands. In 960–61, the Byzantine general Nikiforos Fokas reconquered Crete, but, by the 11th century, the Normans of Sicily and the Venetians were raiding the Ionian islands.

Venetians, Genoese and Crusaders

Venice, with its eye on the Greek islands, encouraged its Frankish allies of the Fourth Crusade to sack Constantinople in 1204. The Venetians then seized Evvoia (Evia), the Ionian islands, Crete and bases on the mainland. The Cyclades became the Duchy of Naxos, ruled by the Venetian Sanudo family, and the Dodecanese were taken by the

Knights of the Order of St John, who also fortified Rhodes and Kos. Genoa acquired the northeast Aegean islands through the marriage of a Genoese prince to a Byzantine princess.

The Turks in the Greek islands

The Turkish conquest of mainland Greece, except for a few Venetian strongholds, was complete by 1460, but the islands held out for much longer. Crete did not fall until 1669 and Tinos held out until 1715. Corfu was threatened, but remained part of the Venetian empire until conquered by France in 1797. Turkish rule was a mixture of brutality and negligence. Many seafarers grew rich on the sea-trade of the Ottoman empire (which the Greeks controlled), but islanders who rebelled against the Sultan were massacred.

The British in the Ionian islands

Britain ousted the French from Corfu in 1814, and the seven Ionian islands remained in British hands until 1864, when they were handed back to Greece.

The Italians in the Dodecanese

Italy seized the Dodecanese from Turkey in 1912, making Rhodes the provincial capital and Leros the eastern base of the Italian navy. The Italians restored the Palace of the Grand Masters and the fortifications of Rhodes and left behind many ornate public buildings. When Italy surrendered in 1943, its Aegean possessions were occupied by the Germans and there were destructive raids by British commandos. It was in 1947 that the Dodecanese at last became part of Greece.

Medieval windmill in Rhodes harbour

Politics

Greece has been a parliamentary democracy since the ousting of the military junta which ruled from 1967–74, with a figurehead president (the ceremonial head of state), an elected prime minister and a 300-member parliament, the Voule. But since the collapse of the Greek economy, culminating in the disintegration of the Papandreou administration in November 2011, there is universal disenchantment with almost all political parties – except, perhaps, for a handful of die-hard leftists.

Among the islands of Greece, local political loyalties run deep. Some islands – notably Lesvos and Ikaria in the northeast Aegean – are noted leftist strongholds. Crete still feels itself to be an island apart, harking back to its brief heyday as a republic in its own right and still loyal to the spirit of Elevtherios Venizelos, the Cretan firebrand republican and the greatest figure of 20th century Greek politics.

Political parties

Two main parties – the centre-left PASOK (Pan Hellenic Socialist Alliance) and the right-wing Nea Dimokratia ('New Democracy') – dominate Greek politics, overshadowing a plethora of smaller left- and right-wing parties. Until the economic troubles that became a full-blown political crisis in 2011, PASOK, led by George Papandreou, seemed to be in control of things, holding 160 parliamentary seats against ND's 91 and KKE's (Greek Communist Party) 21. A rag-tag remainder was divided between the radical-left Syringa coalition, the ultra-conservative nationalist-religious LAOS (Popular Orthodox Rally), and a sprinkling of independent defectors from the two major parties. The political picture, however, changed dramatically in the latter half of 2011.

Trouble in paradise

By 2008 the apparent 'economic miracle' which began with accession to the European Union was being revealed as a sham, with public and private finances afloat on a sea of cheap loans and EU funds. As the economy slowed, unemployment rose and businesses failed. In 2008 there were strikes, demonstrations and riots in Crete and Corfu as well as on the mainland. ND lost the 2009 election, leaving PASOK with a majority in parliament, but also with a poisonous legacy of economic crisis. To secure a multi-billion-euro cash injection from the EU, the European Central Bank and the

International Monetary Fund and save Greece from bankruptcy, the government agreed to a deeply unpopular array of austerity measures, prompting further unrest. In 2011, even taxi drivers went on strike, and there were rumours (which proved to be unfounded) that the government planned to sell some of Greece's uninhabited islands.

The financial bail-out bought the Papandreou administration some breathing space – but not enough. Caught between Greece's EU creditors and an enraged populace, Papandreou threatened a referendum on the cuts, then withdrew the offer. In November 2011 he was forced to resign, and the PASOK administration was replaced by an interim national government led by Loukas Papademos, former governor of the Bank of Greece and former vice-president of the European Central Bank. New elections were tentatively scheduled for May 2012, ahead of yet another EU-led bail-out planned for October 2012.

Greece's future remains uncertain. In a best-case scenario, an austerity programme coupled with a write-off of much of the national debt by Greece's creditors will pull the economy around. In the worst case, Greece may be forced to default completely on its debts, leave the Eurozone, and resign itself to life on the periphery of the EU.

Parliament Building at Syntagma Square, Athens

Culture

Visitors to the islands may still see grain being winnowed on a stone threshing floor and bread being baked in a wood-fired oven. Mules and donkeys are still vital load-carriers for farmers on steep hillsides. The advent of mass tourism, and access to the Internet, satellite TV and mobile phones, have both had an impact on the culture of even the most remote island communities, but each island still retains a clear cultural identity of its own.

These days, though, the grain will not have been ground in an island mill. The surviving windmills in places such as Mikonos have become chic holiday homes, and flour for the bakeries comes from big mills on the mainland.

Boats and planes

Big, fast, modern ferries, high-speed hydrofoils and jet aircraft have taken the place of the caiques and steamers of the old days, bringing the islands closer to the mainland and the outside world. Islands with international airports or domestic flights to Athens are the envy of those without, and charter flights are seen by every islander as the key to a fast tourism fortune.

The tourism boom

Charter flights now go straight to more than a dozen holiday isles from the big cities of Europe, bringing millions of visitors every year to the beaches of their dreams. Islanders who once scraped a bare living from handkerchief-sized fields and thorny goat pasture now grow prosperous from holidaymakers; jobs are created, and there is far more incentive for young islanders to stay at home instead of seeking a livelihood elsewhere. Moribund villages have been reborn and tottering houses rebuilt.

Change for the better?

Have all the changes been positive? Most definitely not. Once-tranquil havens are lined with noisy bars and discos, unsilenced motorbikes boom down narrow streets, and thriving resorts have mushroomed on unspoilt island beaches. The tourism season is mostly summer only, and competition for tourist revenue in peak season can be intense and unseemly.

That said, the islands remain very special. There are still hundreds of spots away from the crowds, and Greek islanders remain among the most charming people in the world. Even on the most developed island, a short journey inland, away from the smell of suntan oil and the beat of the disco, takes you back to villages and landscapes largely unaffected by the holiday boom.

Islanders overseas

Millions of Greeks left their homeland during the 19th century, and many islands which once numbered their inhabitants in tens of thousands have been decimated. Migrants from any one island tended to head for the same destination, and almost all dreamed of returning when their fortunes were made. Not all succeeded, but on Samos and Kithira you will hear lots of Greek-Australian accents; Kalimnos and Halki have links with Florida; Ikaria and Lesvos with the USA and Canada; on Karpathos you may meet Greek returnees from Kenya and Sudan.

Island personality

People who have met Greeks overseas hustling to make their fortune are sometimes surprised to see how laid-back they seem to be in their natural habitat. That is partly because much of the hard work of an island day is done in the early morning hours, when most visitors are still asleep. Partly, too, islanders are blessed with a sunny mentality that takes life as it comes, though they can drive a hard bargain when they want to.

Ancient ancestors?

You may well meet Greeks bearing ancient names – Aristotle and Socrates are popular – but, unsurprisingly, modern Greeks have not much in common with their ancestors of more than 2,000 years ago. There is a real pride in their achievements, but if Greeks do look back on a Hellenic Golden Age, it is the Classical Era as well as the 1,000-year Byzantine empire of Constantine the Great and his heirs.

On smaller, less prosperous islands such as Sikinos, traditional farming methods are still practised

Impressions

You will find relics of the ancient world scattered throughout the islands. Some carefully signposted sites have little more than a few scattered column-drums or foundations to mark them, and all have suffered the ravages of up to 4,000 years of natural disasters, war, invasion and neglect.

Crete and the Aegean island groups offer the richest treasure trove. Sites guaranteed not to disappoint include Knossos, Festos and Gortis on Crete (*see pp80–83*); Lindos, Ialissos and the Temple of Apollo on Rhodes (*see pp108–9*); the Agora on Kos (*see p89*); the Sanctuary of the Great Gods on Samothraki (*see pp126–8*); Akrotiri on Santorini (Thira) (*see p68*); and, perhaps most of all, the complex of shrines and sanctuaries on Delos (*see pp66–7*).

A specialist guidebook or guide who knows the area is vital if you want to make the most of your sightseeing, helping the mind's eye to see the palaces and temples as they once were.

Beaches

The Greek islands offer every kind of beach, from tiny, hard-to-reach coves of white pebbles to sweeps of sand lined with loungers and parasols. There are long sandy beaches on Corfu and its Ionian neighbours, Zakinthos and

Kefalonia, on Paros and Mikonos, on the north coast of Crete, and on Rhodes, Samos and Kos. Santorini (Thira) has beaches of black volcanic sand (which can get painfully hot under the midsummer sun). Best of all, perhaps, is popular Skiathos, with many beaches.

Castles

Venetians, Turks, Genoese and Crusaders left crag-top castles towering over key harbours everywhere. Some, like those on Corfu and Leros, are still used by the Greek military. Among the most impressive are Kithira's Venetian keep, the castles of the Gattelusi on Lesvos, the fortresses of the Knights of St John on Kos and the fortified Monastery of St John the Divine on Patmos.

Historic towns

The Old Town of Rhodes, with its massive fortifications, labyrinth of alleys and restored palace, is the most striking of all the island capitals. Hania and Rethimno on Crete, and the island capital on Kos, are all interesting blends of ancient and medieval history with an exotic whiff of the East. Naxos Town, the capital of Naxos, with its whitewashed, hidden citadel of the Sanudo dukes, is another delight. Corfu Town offers a different history, with reminders of Venice, revolutionary France and Victorian England.

Picturesque villages

The boxy white houses and blue-domed churches of so many postcards are found in the Cyclades group. The island capital almost always bears the name of the island itself, though islanders often just call it Hora (the market-village). The prettiest include the dramatic crater-edge Hora on Santorini (Thira), the harbourside Horas of Mikonos and Paros, and the hilltop Hora of Folegandros. Astipalea and Amorgos are lovely white villages, too.

For a taste of a different village style, visit Molivos on Lesvos with its tall, Turkish-style homes, the Argo-Saronic islands and their sea-captains'

Greek island beaches range from vast sweeps of sand to tiny pebbly coves

Island-hop cheaply by ferry, or more expensively by chartering a yacht

mansions, or Lindos on Rhodes with its pebble-mosaic courtyards.

When to go

The islands are most crowded in July and August. To avoid the crowds and the scorching heat, visit from mid-April to mid-June, or in September and early October. Spring brings the added beauty of red, yellow and purple wild flowers, and in September the sea is still deliciously warm. The weather stays quite balmy into November, but it does become wet and windy. Most tourism facilities close by the end of October, though many smaller, upmarket hotels now stay open all year.

Island to island

The arrival of the ferry is the high point of the day in a harbour village, and as an ant-like parade of backpackers and locals pours off the boat, accompanied by much shouting, gesticulating and sounding of horns from a cavalcade of trucks, cars and motorcycles, chaos seems to reign. In fact, it is all very organised, and, allowing for wind and weather, it is surprising how punctual most ferries are. Timetables change monthly, and it is easy to plan and book inter-island ferries using online resources such as *www.gtp.gr*

Buying a ticket

Harbourside agencies sell tickets, but each agency represents a different line. Where several lines operate, fares will be much the same but schedules differ, and the agency is unlikely to tell you about the services of a competing ferry. Ask around to be sure, or enquire at the Port Police office (*Limenarkion*), where an up-to-date timetable is displayed. Port Police officers wear natty white uniforms. If you plan to island-hop, always allow for delays: strong winds can stop sailing for 24 hours or more and ferry schedules change every month.

Ferry, hydrofoil or catamaran?

Main-line ferries are big, fast and modern, with Pullman-seated lounges available for passengers buying the cheapest fare. Shorter hops may be served by smaller ferries with fewer facilities, but drinks and snacks are always available on board. Hydrofoils and high-speed catamaran ferries are a faster but costlier option on most main routes in summer, offering a smooth and speedy crossing.

Flying

Following its privatisation and merger with former rival Aegean Airlines, Olympic Air (*www.olympicair.com*) enjoys a near-monopoly of domestic aviation, flying to more than 20 islands from mainland airports including Athens and Thessaloniki. There are also some flights between islands. Pre-privatisation, fares were kept low, but are likely to rise sharply due to lack of competition.

Getting around

By bus

Some islands (such as Skiathos and Rhodes) have excellent bus services geared to the needs of tourists. Crete has good long-distance buses serving the entire island. On many other islands, however, bus services are limited or non-existent.

By boat

On the most popular holiday islands, small motorboats ply between the main villages and resorts, and the best beaches. Self-drive motorboats can be hired on some islands.

By car

Cars, beach buggies or 4WD vehicles can be hired almost everywhere. Car hire in Greece is relatively expensive, and soft-top cars cost more. Roads are often rough and care is needed on the many sharp bends and steep hills. Make sure your vehicle insurance covers all damage (though damage to the underside and to tyres will always be your responsibility).

By bike

Bikes are available for hire on some islands and are ideal for short trips. Longer journeys can be hilly and hot.

Hitchhiking

Islanders are quite generous with rides, but you may have to wait if it's quiet.

By moped and motorcycle

Thousands of holidaymakers are injured, and some are killed, each year, riding rented motorcycles. Always wear a helmet, even if the renter claims it is not necessary. Island roads and island traffic are dangerous to the inexperienced rider. If you have not ridden before, it is not advisable to start here.

By taxi

Taxis are quite cheap and are a very useful way of getting around. They await each ferry and are quickly snapped up. Be first ashore (you'll have to be pushy!) to be sure of getting one. Sharing with others is not unusual.

Manners and customs

Island hospitality is legendary. Away from the boom-town resorts, you may be surprised by a carafe of retsina sent to your table by a complete stranger, or a gift of fruit from an island orchard. However, in the most popular resorts *philoxenia* ('love of guests') is vanishing, though slowly, as the tourism-profit motive asserts itself.

Queuing

Queuing for transport is unheard of. Boarding a bus or a ferry is a race for seats, and disembarking is a scramble for waiting taxis. In banks or post offices queues do form, though some Greeks will still push in ahead of tourists.

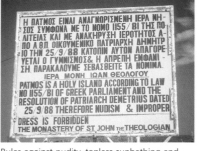

Rules against nudity, topless sunbathing and 'improper dress' are more often ignored than obeyed

Dress code

Topless sunbathing is now accepted on even the most public beaches. Nudity, however, is illegal. It is sanctioned on designated beaches, but it may offend on many town or resort beaches. Shorts and T-shirts are acceptable summer wear everywhere, but knees and arms must be covered when visiting monasteries.

Women travellers

Greek men nearly always feel that a woman is flattered by their attention, but an unambiguous 'no' is usually a sufficient deterrent to would-be Romeos. You are much more likely to be harassed by foreign visitors than by islanders.

Language

The Greek language and alphabet can be intimidating, but a little Greek goes a very long way. Greeks believe that their language is almost impossible for foreigners to learn and knowledge of a few simple phrases will be extravagantly praised. English and German are widely spoken by islanders as a result of tourism, emigration and service in the merchant navy.

Islanders use plenty of body language, which can be helpful or confusing. A backward jerk of the head, which looks like a nod, is actually a 'no', accompanied for emphasis by a click of the tongue. A rapid side-to-side shake of the head means anything from 'I don't understand' to 'What can I do for you?'

Peace and beauty can be found in the most unexpected places

Ionian islands

Known in Greek as the Eptanisa ('Seven Islands'), the Ionian islands stretch in a chain down Greece's west coast, from Corfu in the north to Kithira, all by itself off the southern tip of the Peloponnese. Some of the country's best sandy beaches are to be found on these shores, and landscapes are greener and easier on the eye than those of many Aegean islands.

CORFU (Kerkira)

Corfu is an island of rolling green farmland, vineyards and orange groves, all under the looming bulk of Mt Pantokrator, gazing eastward across a narrow strait to the bare mountainsides of Albania seemingly only a stone's throw away. Corfu is the second largest of the Ionian islands (after Kefalonia) and is by far the most popular with visitors, with resorts on every beach along its 217km (135-mile) coastline. Corfu caters to visitors of all kinds, from plutocrats who rent private villas or moor their mega-yachts around Nissaki on its northeast coast to downmarket package holidaymakers who throng the sandy beaches, pubs and open-air dance clubs of spots such as Kavos, on the southern tip of the island, or Benitses and Ipsos on the east coast. The island capital, with a pretty town centre that shows the influences of the many centuries of Venetian rule, is now a UNESCO World Heritage Site, and inland – away from the busy beaches – the island's farming villages, rural landscapes, vineyards and olive groves are also quite untouched, as are the wooded slopes of the Pantokrator massif.

Corfu's busiest resorts are on the east coast – closest to the island capital and its airport – but the most spectacular beaches, the prettiest scenery and the finest sunsets are on the west coast, where you'll also, surprisingly, find plenty of space and solitude on long stretches of sandy shore.

Corfu is shaped like a hammer, with a broad 'head' at its northern end and a crooked, thinner 'handle'. Mt Pantokrator dominates the north, with its bald, grey 960m (2,972ft) summit rising from thickly wooded slopes.

Corfu was part of the Byzantine empire from the 4th century AD, was seized by Venice in 1205 and stayed in Venetian hands, resisting several Turkish assaults, until 1797, when it was conquered by France. In 1814, France was ousted by Britain, and in

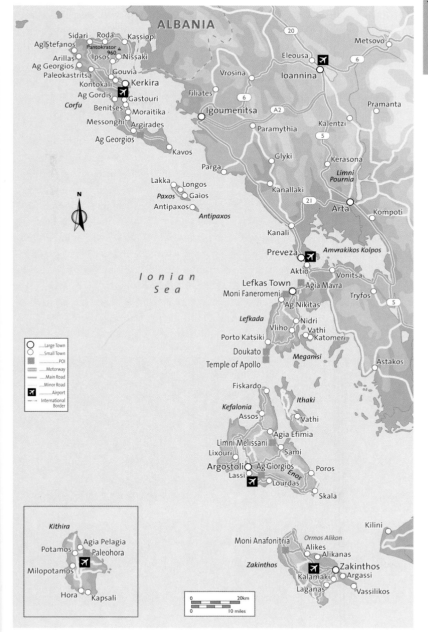

1815 the island (and the rest of the Ionian) became a British protectorate. The Union Flag was hauled down in 1864, when the islands joined the Kingdom of Greece. The Venetians left an Italianate island capital, the French bestowed a stylish arcade of shops and cafés on Corfu Town, and the British legacy includes a collection of grand public buildings and a taste for cricket and ginger beer.

Kerkira (Corfu Town)

Corfu's charming capital looks quite different from most island villages. In fact, its appearance is Italianate rather than typically Greek, with its faded rose and ochre stucco buildings, complete with wooden shutters, wrought-iron balconies and flights of stone steps connecting dozens of tiny *piazzas*. The

picturesque Campiello quarter was built during the Venetian era, on a headland guarded by two fortresses: the Paleo Frourio (Old Fortress) on an eastern crag, and the Nea Frourio (New Fortress) to the north, near the harbour. Grand public buildings erected during the French and British occupations of the 19th century stand around the Spianada park on the east side of the old town, and a ring of modern outer suburbs surrounds the historic centre. The focal point of the old town is the Spianada, an elegant square where cricket is still played on a huge lawn and military bands play on summer evenings at a bandstand built by the British. On one side of the square is the main French contribution to local architecture, a Parisian-style arcade of stylish cafés known as the

Corfu's shabby but picturesque Old Town is a UNESCO World Heritage Site

A vividly coloured icon of the sainted Byzantine empress Theodora adorns Corfu's cathedral

Liston. Overlooking the lawns is a statue of Ioannis Capodistrias (1776–1831), Greece's first president.

Achillion Palace

This opulent royal estate overlooking Corfu Town is the most spectacular sight on the island, redolent of the belle époque of the 19th century, when Corfu began to become a retreat for the crowned heads and aristocrats of Europe, among them the Empress Elisabeth (nicknamed 'Sissi') of Austria, who built this grandiose neoclassical palace as a holiday home. After her death, it passed into the hands of Kaiser Wilhelm II. The flamboyant palace, its elegantly landscaped grounds, and its collection of art and antiques became state property.
*Gastouri. Tel: (26610) 56210.
Open: Apr–Oct daily 8am–7pm;
Nov–Mar daily 9am–3.30pm.
Admission charge.*

Agios Spiridon

The island's patron saint, whose embalmed, silver-encased body is preserved here and paraded through the streets on ceremonial occasions, is credited with warding off the plague in 1630, seeing off the Turkish invasion of 1716, and even protecting the town from Italian bombers during World War II. The church has a remarkable, elaborately painted ceiling.
*Platia Agias Spiridou. Open: daily.
Free admission.*

Arkheologiko Moussio (Archaeological Museum)

Highlights of this museum's collection of finds from local archaeological sites include a 7th-century BC stone lion and an effigy of the terrifying Gorgon from the Temple of Artemis.
*Vraila 5. Tel: (26610) 30680.
www.odysseus.culture.gr. Open: Tue–Sun
8.30am–3pm. Admission charge.*

Byzantino Moussio (Byzantine Museum)

Housed in a 15th-century church, this museum features colourful icons dating from the 15th to the 19th centuries, along with other Orthodox religious artefacts.

Panagia tis Antivouniotissas, Arseniou 3. Tel: (26610) 38313. Open: Apr–Oct Tue–Sun 8am–7pm; Nov–Mar Tue–Sun 8.30am–2.30pm. Admission charge (same ticket as Asiatic Art Museum).

Kanoni, Vlaherna and Pontikonisi

A short causeway connects the delightful island monastery of Vlaherna with the Kanoni peninsula (so-called because a battery of French cannon was sited here during the Napoleonic Wars). Just offshore lies the famous Pontikonisi ('Mouse Island'), which appears on so many postcards of Corfu.

4km (2 1/2 miles) south of town centre. Open: daily.

Mitropoli

The cathedral in the old quarter, built in 1577, houses the coffin of the Byzantine empress Theodora, who was canonised in the 9th century.

Platia Mitropoleos. Open: daily. Free admission.

Mon Repos Palace
(Palaiopolis Museum)

Built for the British High Commissioner, Frederic Adam, in 1824, this grand villa became the Greek family's summer residence and is the birthplace of Prince Philip, the Duke of Edinburgh. The restored villa is now the very attractive Palaiopolis Museum, and contains some fine paintings and antiques as well as finds from Corfu's key archaeological sites. It stands on the site of the ancient town of Kerkyra, and in its landscaped grounds are the remains of temples to Hera, Apollo and Poseidon.

Palaiopolis, Dimokratias, between Corfu Town and airport. Tel: (26610) 41369. Open: May–Oct 8am–7.30pm. Palace and grounds free, charge for museum.

Moussio Solomos (Solomos Museum)

The former home of the venerated Greek poet Dionysos Solomos (1786–1857), with its collection of manuscripts and memorabilia, is only of very minor interest to most non-Greek visitors.

Arseniou 41. Tel: (26610) 30674. Open: Jun–Aug daily 9.30am–2pm; Sept–May daily 9.30am–1pm. Admission charge.

Museum of Asiatic Art
(Palace of St Michael and St George)

This elegant 19th-century palace was built for the British high commissioners of the Ionian islands and was later used by the Greek monarchy. It now houses a collection of artefacts from the Middle East and Asia.

North end of Spianada. Tel: (26610) 30443. Open: May–Oct Tue–Sun 8.30am–7pm; Nov–Apr Tue–Sun 8.30am–3pm. Admission charge.

Nea Frourio (New Fortress)

This angular stone fortress, built between the 16th and 19th centuries, is 'new' only by comparison with the 'old' Paleo Frourio. Parts of it are still used by the Greek navy, and it also contains a ceramics museum and a café-bar.

Open: Tue–Sun 8.30am–3pm. Admission charge.

The beautiful Corfu coastline

Paleo Frourio (Old Fortress)

This stronghold, built in the 16th century, stands on twin crags which are severed from the city by a sea moat. There are fine views from its highest turret, and on summer evenings it is used for dramatic sound and light performances. Also within its walls are a Venetian prison, built in 1786, a British barracks and hospital buildings dating from 1850, and a classical church of Agios Georgios (St George), built in 1840.

Access by bridge from east of the Spianada. Open: May–Oct Tue–Sun 8.30am–7pm. Admission charge.

Benitses

The closest resort to the airport, Benitses is virtually a beach suburb of Corfu Town. Overwhelmingly dominated by British tourists in summer, it is the epitome of cheap and cheerful holidaymaking, with a parade of bars advertising UK sports TV, restaurants advertising 'English breakfast', and tacky souvenir shops, while inland lie dozens of purpose-built hotels and apartment complexes.

13km (8 miles) south of the centre of Corfu Town.

Moraitika and Messonghi

These two villages have merged together into one stretch of bars, tavernas and hotels, similar in character to Benitses.

9km (6 miles) south of Benitses.

Kavos

Close to the island's southern tip, Kavos is Corfu's party beach. Dozens of music bars and several large dance clubs line its streets and beachfront, and many of its (mainly British) patrons slumber most of the day on the sand before waking up at sundown for yet another night of partying. The beach is long, with shallow warm water, and stretches all the way south to Asprokavos, the

Ionian islands

southern tip of Corfu. As well as nightlife, Kavos also offers a wide range of powered and non-powered watersports and 'adrenalin activities' such as bungee jumping, plus day trips by boat to Corfu's smaller neighbour, Paxi (Paxos).

Approximately 40km (25 miles) south of Corfu Town.

Kontokali and Gouvia

Heading up the east coast from Corfu town, the first resort you come to is Kontokali. It's a lot newer than most of its east-coast rivals, having taken to tourism only since the building of a new marina a few years ago. Its clientele is more multinational than many of its British-dominated neighbours, and it even attracts a sprinkling of Greek weekenders from Corfu Town and holidaymakers from the mainland. The Blue-Flag-rated beach is sandy and well-kept. Less than 800m (900yds) north, Gouvia is solidly back into mass-market tourism, with plenty of places to eat, drink and party.

9km (6 miles) north of Corfu Town.

Ipsos and Dassia

Ipsos and Dassia almost merge, with two long stretches of beach separated only by a low, wooded headland occupied by a couple of hotels. Of the two, Dassia is closest to Corfu Town, is a little more cosmopolitan and has the better beach – a long stretch of shingle fringing a bay which is great for watersports. Ipsos, less than 1km (2/3 mile) to the north, is a long ribbon of bars, shops, restaurants and tavernas with plenty of small hotels along a narrow beach that is little more than a stretch of pebbles beside the main coast road. An enterprising local council trucks in tons of sand dredged from the seabed to make the beach more attractive in summer. At the south end of town, a tiny harbour is a reminder of Ipsos's roots as a fishing village. Both resorts boast an array of nightlife from displays of 'traditional' Greek dancing accompanied by plate-smashing to dance clubs and music bars blasting out the latest imported sounds.

16km (10 miles) north of Corfu Town.

Nissaki

The poshest villas and holiday homes in Corfu (which are some of the poshest in the Mediterranean) are hidden around the small village of Nissaki and along the stretch of coast which bulges eastward towards Albania. There are no big beaches here, so it's the most peaceful part of the east coast – if you can afford it. Many of the luxurious villas here come complete with motor-boats, so you can explore the small coves along the coast or cruise to Nissaki or Kassiopi for lunch or dinner.

8km (5 miles) north of Ipsos.

Kassiopi

The looming, bare mountains of Albania look close enough to touch from the rocky headland beyond Kassiopi's pretty little harbour, where the ruins of a Venetian castle indicate a

turbulent past. The fine, almost lagoon-like harbour made Kassiopi the most important village in northern Corfu, and although it is crammed with day-trippers in high summer, it is much more peaceful than most east-coast resorts after dark and at weekends, and is certainly more sophisticated, with some upmarket restaurants by the harbour and pleasant small hotels, as well as villas in the nearby countryside.
30km (19 miles) north of Corfu Town.

Roda

Midway along the north coast of the island, Roda has one of the best beaches in the area. Discovered by tourism in the 1980s, it grew quickly into a rather sprawling resort, but has mellowed and matured since then. Roda is surrounded by vineyards, olive groves and farmland, and with its calm, shallow water, the long sand-and-pebble beach makes it a favourite family resort. It's also an excellent base for active travellers who want to explore the northern part of the island, with good walking (ranging from gentle strolls through the fields to hikes to the top of nearby Pantokrator), pony-trekking, 4WD excursions and watersports.
37km (23 miles) northwest of Corfu Town.

Mount Pantokrator (Pantokrator Oros)

Corfu's highest mountain, which dominates the northeast part of the island, can be reached from several directions, but Roda, Kassiopi and Ipsos are the best starting points for a day's exploring. You can drive almost all the way to the top (a 4WD vehicle is not essential), leaving your car at Petaleia village to walk the last 2km (1¼ miles) on a rough footpath. For a more energetic, but prettier, ascent (taking 60–90 minutes each way) start at the picturesquely dilapidated hamlet of Perithia. The superb panorama encompasses the whole of the island, as well as the treeless mountains of Albania to the east and the Pindos ranges sloping off to the south on the Greek mainland.
25–30km (16–19 miles) north of Corfu Town.

Sidari

Like Roda, Sidari has grown into a laid-back beach resort, though it also has plenty of nightlife in the shape of music bars and dance venues. It has a long beach of dark sand and warm, shallow water.

Sidari has expanded westward from its original beach core to embrace the long, rocky inlet lined by weirdly eroded cliffs known as the Canal d'Amour, about 2km (1¼ miles) west of Sidari beach. A dip in its waters guarantees any young woman will meet the man of her dreams – at least, according to local legend. A suburb of new hotels and apartments has grown up its banks, and is known as Canal d'Amour Village, with its own stretch of beach.
48km (30 miles) northwest of Corfu Town.

Agios Stefanos and Arillas

At the northern end of Corfu's west coast, the west-facing bay of Agios Stefanos has a huge sweep of fine, pale-yellow sand and is one of the best places on Corfu to watch the sun set. Even in high season, the beach is uncrowded (at least by Corfu standards). There are several tavernas and a couple of music bars for late-nighters. Arillas, the next bay to the south, is separated from Agios Stefanos by a headland and has another strand of sand and pebbles, more village tavernas and a plethora of powered and unpowered watersports.
On the northwestern tip of the island.

Agios Georgios (north)

Confusingly, there are two beaches called Agios Georgios on Corfu's west coast. This one has an 8km (5-mile) crescent of golden sand and pebbles stretching all the way round a south-facing bay. Agios Georgios village is midway along this curve of beach, backed by olive groves and citrus plantations, and offers cafés, bars, tavernas and watersports.
Midway between Arillas and Paleokastritsa.

Paleokastritsa

Paleokastritsa has been a noted beauty spot since the British occupation, luring artists including Edward Lear, the comic poet and painter (1812–88), who made many watercolour sketches of local landscapes and people. Nowadays,

however, artists are way outnumbered by holidaymakers, some of whom stay in villas and guesthouses, while others are day-trippers. Steep, pine-wooded slopes and limestone crags surround this gorgeous double bay. Its two small beaches become crowded during the day, but you can take a motorboat from the village jetty to quieter coves and beaches nearby.
26km (16 miles) northwest of Corfu Town.

Zoodochos Pigi Monastery

This fortress-like 18th-century monastery guards a supposedly miracle-working, 12th-century icon of the Virgin. The rock that can be seen on the horizon is said to be a pirate ship which was turned to stone by the Virgin to protect her monastery.
Agios Nikolaos promontory.
Open: daily. Admission charge (candle purchase obligatory).

Angelokastro

It's worth visiting the ruin of this small castle tower on a giddy peak above the sea just for the view. It is named after Michael I Angelos, the 13th-century Byzantine despot who ordered it to be built, and within its tumbledown walls is a tiny whitewashed chapel.
11km (7 miles) north of Paleokastritsa. Freely accessible.

Agios Gordis

Agios Gordis is one of Corfu's finest beaches. It is very popular with

watersports enthusiasts, but it has not yet blossomed into a full-scale holiday resort along the lines of those on the east coast. The beach, which nestles at the foot of a dramatic range of coastal hills covered in tall, elegant pine trees, is a mix of yellow sand and clean shingle, shelving into crystal-clear waters.
16km (10 miles) southwest of Corfu Town.

Agios Georgios (south)

This Agios Georgios is closer to the island capital and the airport than its northern namesake, and inevitably is more developed – it is only 4km (2½ miles) from the busy east-coast strip. That said, despite the pell-mell development at its core – below the farming village of Argirades, about 1km (⅔ mile) inland and uphill – there is still plenty of space on this long stretch of coastline. Just north of the resort is one of Corfu's last stretches of wild coastline, where a spit of sand dunes shelters the brackish Korission lagoon, which teems with flocks of migrating waterbirds, including storks and pelicans, in early spring and autumn.
24km (15 miles) southwest of Corfu Town.

PAXOS (Paxi)

Paxos is among the smallest of the Ionian islands, and the closest to Corfu, so it is a popular day-trip destination. With an area of only 25sq km (10sq miles), it is nevertheless home

OLIVES AND ISLANDERS

The silvery leaves of olive trees seem to cover almost every square metre of Paxos. Olives are part of Greece's heritage, grown from the earliest times as part of the 'Mediterranean triad' which also included grapes and grain. Olive trees are very long-lived and are valuable heirlooms. Like earmarks on sheep, numbers and initials painted on the trunk identify the owner of the tree. A family may have dozens of trees scattered in ones and twos all over an island.

Trees are often owned independently of the land they grow on, and the landowner must allow access for harvesting and pruning. The olive tree yields more fruit if pruned annually, and the slow-burning trimmings make excellent winter firewood. In the old days, islanders made bowls, plates and spoons from close-grained olive wood, which is still used in boat-building.

to around 2,400 islanders, scattered among three coastal villages and around 30 tiny hamlets. The island is almost entirely covered in olive trees – some 300,000 of them, giving plenty of shade for walkers. Most of the island's beaches are tiny and pebbly, dotted at frequent intervals around a 25km (16-mile) shoreline. Mark Antony and Cleopatra are said to have spent their last night together here in 31 BC before sailing to defeat by the forces of the Roman Emperor Octavian (later Augustus) at the sea-battle of Aktion (Actium) 100km (64 miles) south of Paxos just off the mainland.
Paxos is about 20km (12 miles) south of Corfu and 25km (16 miles) west of Parga on the mainland.

Gaios

Paxos's main village, at the southern end of the island, is home to around 1,200 people. This perfect Italianate island capital is built around a flagstoned square on the waterside, overlooked by the bell tower of a graceful church. A narrow channel separates it from two islets, Panagia and Agios Nikolaos, which create a perfect sheltered anchorage, making Gaios a favourite port of call for yacht flotillas.
Facing northeast, near the southern end of the island.

Longos

Longos sits on an east-facing, mirror-calm natural harbour where a handful of villas and cafés crowd around the village square and a narrow quayside from which tables have to be moved when the daily bus wants to squeeze by. There are clean, pebbly coves to the south of the village.
10km (6 miles) north of Gaios.

Lakka

Gentle morning breezes and strong, constant afternoon winds make

Gaios is one of the prettiest places on Paxos

Lakka's pebbly beach and bay one of Greece's premier windsurfing training centres. The village's natural harbour is sheltered by two curving promontories, and the beach is arguably the best on Paxos.
12km (7 miles) northwest of Gaios.

ANTIPAXOS (Antipaxi)

This tiny settlement achieves the startling feat of making its bigger neighbour look both busy and cosmopolitan. Fewer than 50 people live on the island, cultivating small, terraced vineyards, and a handful of tavernas make a good living in summer from day-trippers who come by boat from Corfu, Parga and Paxos. The beach at Vrikes, with its white sand, is crowded when the boats come in, but for a bit more solitude you can easily walk to a clutch of quiet pebble-and-sand coves on Antipaxos's south coast.
5km (3 miles) south of Paxos.

LEFKADA (Lefkas/Levkas)

Lefkada means 'white', and the bare mountain slopes of the hinterland are indeed whitish, with only a few pine trees clinging to their higher flanks. Around and below the central mountains, Lefkada is a verdant, pretty island, with fertile farmland and hundreds of blue beehives scattered among the goat pasture.

Only 650m (2,133ft) separate Lefkada from the mainland, and the narrow strait is crossed by a swing bridge and a causeway guarded by fortifications.

The east coast of the island faces on to a broad, calm expanse of water sheltered by the mainland and the offshore island of Meganisi. Skorpios, one of the tiny wooded islets here, was the former hideaway of the millionaire Onassis family. This is a favourite area for yachts and windsurfers.

The west coast is more rugged, with cliffs and steep slopes rising above a string of white sandy beaches formed by the pounding of winter storms.

In the turbulent Middle Ages, Lefkada changed hands even more frequently than most Greek islands. It was fought over by the Normans of Sicily and the Byzantine empire in the 11th century, taken by the Venetians in 1331, and ruled by Angevin Franks from 1362 until 1467, when it became the only Ionian island to be occupied by the Ottoman Turks. In 1684 it was reconquered by Venice, and from then on shared the fortunes of its Ionian neighbours, with a brief interval of Russian control between 1807 and 1814.
35km (22 miles) from Aktio airport, 40km (25 miles) southwest of the mainland port of Preveza.

Agios Nikitas

There are excellent beaches on either side of this tiny fishing village and resort. Small boats commute between Agios Nikitas and its satellite beaches several times a day in summer.
On the west coast, 8km (5 miles) southwest of Lefkas Town.

The west coast of Lefkada

Doukato (Petra Lefkas)

The legendary poetess Sappho (*c.* 600 BC) is said to have thrown herself from this dramatic 70m (230ft)-high white cliff, as the victim of unrequited love. Traces of a 7th-century BC Temple of Apollo can be seen next to the lighthouse on the island's southern tip.

46km (29 miles) south of Lefkas Town.

Lefkas Town

Levelled by the 1953 earthquake, Lefkas Town has been patchily rebuilt and has an eccentric charm. The upper storeys of many houses are built of brightly painted corrugated iron (an anti-earthquake ploy). The town faces inland, away from its lagoon, and hardly feels like a harbour town. Instead, it is more like an inland farming village. Repeated earthquakes have left it with little of historic interest, but a medieval castle and monastery lie nearby.

Northwest coast.

Agia Mavra

The 14th-century fortress of the Orsinis has ramparts built in 1807 by the Russians, who briefly occupied Lefkas between the ousting of France and the British takeover.

1km (²/₃ mile) from Lefkas Town, on the islet midway along the causeway.

Moni Faneromeni (Faneromeni Monastery)

This deserted monastery dates from the 16th century and still possesses its wooden simantron, the heavy wooden bar beaten with a hammer to call the monks to prayer.

3km (2 miles) southwest of Lefkas Town on the road to Agios Nikitas.

Nidri (Nydri)

Midway down the east coast, Nydri stands on a mirror-like lagoon which is punctuated by tree-tufted islands and, in summer, covered with the white and Day-Glo sails of yachts and windsurfers. There are some pleasant walks in the hilly farming country inland, and a long narrow beach stretches in front of the village.

17km (11 miles) southwest of Lefkas Town.

Porto Katsiki

One of the most spectacular beaches in all the islands, this white crescent of coarse sand lies beneath a half-circle of jagged cliffs. It can be reached by a rough, nerve-racking jeep ride or, more comfortably, by boat from Agios Nikitas.

40km (25 miles) southwest of Lefkas Town.

MEGANISI

Tadpole-shaped Meganisi lies just off the southeast coast of Lefkada, and despite its small size it is home to almost 1,000 people, who live in scattered farms and in two harbour villages – Vathi and Spartohori – and one little hill village, Katomeri, the island's capital. Miniature beaches are dotted around its coastline, at Spilia, Fanari, Atherinos, Limonari and Agios Ioannis, which is the best known and has at least one summer taverna and great views across to Lefkada. At Spilia, near the tip of the island's 'tail', the second-largest sea-cave in Greece is the most impressive sight on the island.

Meganisi is 4km (2½ miles) southeast of Nidri on Lefkada.

KEFALONIA (Cephalonia/Kefallonia)

The largest of the Ionian islands, Kefalonia is a semi-tropical study in vivid turquoise and ultramarine seas, a palette of green woodland shades, and brilliant white limestone cliffs and pebble beaches.

Tourism has boomed here (more recently than in neighbouring isles) – partly sparked by exposure in the novel *Captain Corelli's Mandolin*, by Louis de Bernières, and the film version, starring Nicolas Cage, which tells the story of a love affair set against the Italian occupation of the island during World War II. There is a world of difference between northern Kefalonia, where a few small seaside villages huddle beneath steep slopes, and the more populous south coast, with a string of low-key resort villages scattered along sand-and-pebble beaches east of the airport and the island capital, Argostoli.

On the northwest coast, vertiginous limestone cliffs loom over white beaches (Mirtos is a must-see, but the drive there is not for the nervous) and the most brilliantly coloured blue sea in the Ionian. Inland, Kefalonia rises to the 1,628m (5,291ft) summit of Oros (Mt) Enos, which dominates the southern half of the island. The highest slopes of the massif are treeless, but its lower flanks are wooded and the fertile lands below are covered with citrus orchards, olive groves and vineyards. Rombola wine, made on Kefalonia, is rated among the best in Greece. A deep bight, the Gulf of Argostoli, separates the larger part of the island from the oddly shaped Paliki peninsula, which holds little of interest to the average holidaymaker.

With a couple of honourable exceptions at Assos and Fiskardo, Kefalonia's towns and villages look surprisingly modern and functional. Along with its neighbouring islands, Kefalonia was clobbered by the 1953 earthquake. Few buildings survived, and islanders took the opportunity to build modern communities from the ground up. The result isn't as picturesque as visitors might expect, but as usual bougainvillea, potted plants and palm trees do much to soften the lines of newer buildings.

Argostoli

Kefalonia's capital is on a fine natural anchorage. A 650m (2,133ft) causeway (built by British engineers in the 19th century) crosses the mouth of this lagoon, which in spring and autumn is a birdwatcher's paradise, attracting storks, pelicans and other migrant birds. Argostoli is a surprisingly stylish little town, with a recently refurbished (and mainly car-free) centre that owes little to tourism, and where some great traditional cafés favoured by older citizens sit next to flashy café-bars populated by their designer-dressed grandchildren.

Arxaioloyiko Mouseio (Archaeological Museum)

This museum, in the centre of Argostoli, contains a modest collection of ceramics, bronzes, marbles and other finds from archaeological sites around the island.
Vergoti 89. Tel: (26710) 28300.
Open: Tue–Sun 8.30am–3pm.
Admission charge.

Mouseio Koryialeniou (Korgialenos Museum)

The exhibits here are much more recent – and much more interesting – than those in the nearby Archaeological Museum, and include traditional costumes, paintings, maps and prints, and re-creations of rooms in grand Venetian mansions, peasant homes and artisans' workshops.
Zervou 12. Tel: (26710) 28835.
Open: Apr–Oct Mon–Sat 9am–3pm.
Admission charge.

Agia Efimia

This dinky, slightly ramshackle fishing harbour has a few small guesthouses and family-run hotels, a scattering of surprisingly good places to eat, and is the base for several scuba-diving and boat-rental outfits. Its main importance, however, is as the port for shuttle ferries to Ithaki (Ithaca), only a couple of kilometres away on the eastern horizon.

About 31km (20 miles) northeast of Argostoli.

Agios Giorgios

The hilltop fortress of Agios Giorgios (St George) stands guard over southern Kefalonia. Built in 1300 by the Orsini clan (the island's Venetian rulers), it was their capital until 1757, when they relocated to Argostoli. Apart from the ruined shells of houses and a few churches, little survives within its crumbling ramparts to indicate that 15,000 people once lived here, but the view of a patchwork of orchards, olive groves and vineyards stretching down to the sea is fantastic.

About 31km (20 miles) southeast of Argostoli.

Assos

Tiny Assos, on the west coast, with fewer than 100 inhabitants, is the perfect spot for a quiet island holiday. Small guesthouses and hotels are scattered around its hilly streets, and a dozen or so bars and tavernas stand along its quayside and a small crescent of pebbly beach. The village stands beside

A café just off the main square in Argostoli

an almost landlocked natural harbour, overlooked by a steep crag which is crowned by the ruined battlements of a formidable 16th-century Venetian fortress. Small motorboats can be hired to explore the nearby bays and beaches. *About 32km (20 miles) north of Argostoli.*

Fiskardo

With its harbourfront lined with pastel-coloured houses, smart quayside restaurants and café bars, and a harbour crammed with enviable yachts, Fiskardo has become Kefalonia's postcard-pretty tourism icon. One of the few spots on the island to survive both the 1953 earthquake and the tourism invasion that began in the 1990s more or less intact, it is beginning to show signs of becoming a victim of its own success, with tiers of new villas and stylish hotels rising on the hillsides above it. So far, happily, development has been kept small-scale, but Fiskardo is definitely the priciest and most pretentious place on Kefalonia, as well as the prettiest. Unless you have a yacht at your disposal, it's also hard to get to, requiring a long drive (about 90 minutes from the airport) over increasingly precipitous cliffside roads.
Close to the northern tip of the island, 53km (33 miles) from Argostoli.

Lassi

Just south of Argostoli and only minutes from the airport, Lassi has the best and most accessible sandy beaches on the island and has inevitably developed into Kefalonia's busiest and most extensively equipped resort, with hotels, bars and restaurants lining the sands of Makris Yialos and Platis Yialos beaches.
2km (1½ miles) south of Argostoli, 8km (5 miles) north of the airport.

Limni Melissani (Melissani Cave)

Centuries ago, the roof of this vast, natural limestone cavern collapsed, revealing a subterranean blue pool, lit by sunlight from above and fed by natural tunnels that stretch far beneath the island. Small rowing boats take you into the pool, which seems to glow with turquoise light.

Other caverns nearby have also been opened up: the Drogaritis Cave, near Haliotata (5km south of Sami), is a 15-million-year-old grotto noted for its rare red stalactites.
3km (2 miles) northwest of Sami, on the east coast. Access to caves by boat. Open: daily 8am–sunset. Admission charge.

Lourdas

Lourdas, midway along the south coast of the island, has a long beach of sand and pebbles. Dotted along the beach are a few bar-restaurants and small guesthouses. More places to eat and stay can be found in the small hillside village of Lourdata, about 1km (²/₃ mile) inland from Lourdas.
20km (12 miles) east of Argostoli.

Poros

This port village on the east coast of the island handles ferries and hydrofoils from Killini on the mainland and, in summer, to Zakinthos, Kefalonia's southern neighbour. Unless you're planning to travel on, however, there's really no reason to hang about here.
About 40km (25 miles) east of Argostoli.

Sami

Sami, midway along Kefalonia's east coast, is the island's main seaport, with several sailings daily to Patra on the mainland (from which you can catch a train or bus to Athens). With a handful of places to stay and more than enough places to eat, it's a mostly modern town – though it stood in for Argostoli as the location for the film version of *Captain Corelli's Mandolin*. It was mostly rebuilt after the 1953 earthquake, and a row of palm trees along its seafront helps to mellow its rough edges.

ITHAKI (Ithaca)

Tiny Ithaki (just under 100sq km/39sq miles) is best known as the legendary home of Odysseus (Ulysses) and his goal in his long journey home from the siege of Troy. Another famous visitor, Lord Byron (1788–1824), was so charmed by the island that he toyed with the idea of buying it.

Ithaki is a narrow island, about 20km (12 miles) long from north to south and cut almost in two by the Kolpos Molou (Gulf of Molos). This opening on the east coast has sheltered waters and steady breezes which make the island a delight for dinghy-sailing, windsurfing and other watersports. The island's sand-and-pebble beaches are small but uncrowded and usually clean.
2km (1¼ miles) east of Kefalonia.

Vathi

Ithaki's capital, home to over 2,000 of its 3,600 people, was rebuilt after the 1953 earthquake. Its charm owes more to its superbly scenic site, on a near-landlocked inlet surrounded by steep hills, than to any architectural merit.
At the inner end of a southern arm of the Gulf of Molos.

Marmarospilia (Caves of the Nymphs)

Odysseus is said to have hidden his treasure in this limestone sea-cavern.
3km (2 miles) southwest of Ithaki Town.

Sarakiniko and Skinos

The best beaches on Ithaki are between these headlands on the east coast, reached on foot or by small boats from Ithaki Town.
2–5km (1¼–3 miles) northeast of Ithaki Town.

ZAKINTHOS (Zakynthos/Zante)

After Corfu, Zakinthos is the most popular of the Ionian holiday islands, and it is not difficult to see why. Inland, the island is a pastoral chequerboard of green vineyards, fruit orchards and groves of almonds, grain fields and pastureland. In spring, when its hills and roadsides are ablaze with wild blooms, it is easy to see why the Venetians called it *Fior di Levante* – the Flower of the Levant.

Argassi

The popularity of this crowded resort is hard to explain, as its beach, a narrow strip of sand mixed with shingle, does not come up to the standard of other sunbathing stretches on Zakinthos. However, there are lots of bars and tavernas, and several discos, which gives Argassi a nightlife that runs noisy Laganas a close second. *About 3.6km (2¼ miles) southeast of Zakinthos Town.*

Laganas

Zakinthos's southeast coast is a broad bight, with Kolpos Lagana (the Laganas Gulf) bounded by two rocky headlands, Akr Marathia in the southwest and Akr Geraki in the east. Midway between the two is the tourism boom town of Laganas, which in a few years has grown from a tiny collection of fishermen's cottages to a thriving resort full of hotels, tavernas and bars. East of Laganas, a superb sandy beach stretches for almost 4km (2½ miles) to Kalamaki, a smaller resort spread out among fields behind the beach. Inland, a fertile triangular plain, enclosed by wooded hills to the north, stretches east and west. *10km (6 miles) southwest of Zakinthos Town.*

TURTLES ON THE BRINK

The sandy beaches of many Greek islands are as attractive to marine turtles as they are to visitors. Sadly, nesting turtles and sun-seeking tourists don't coexist well. Female turtles, which lay their eggs in early summer, may be injured by speedboats and jet-skis, vehicles and walkers; sunloungers and the steel poles of parasols crush buried eggs; and the bright lights of seaside resorts disorient newly hatched turtles trying to reach the sea. Part of Laganas Bay on Zakinthos has been declared a reserve, and powerboats are banned from travelling at speed in a large sector of the bay – a ban which is often ignored. The number of loggerhead turtles nesting at Laganas has fallen by more than half since the advent of mass tourism in the 1970s. To give them a chance of survival, follow these rules:

- No lights or noise on nesting beaches at night
- Don't drop litter
- Don't put parasols on dry sand where turtles nest
- Don't try to help hatchlings reach the sea – doing it themselves is vital to their development
- Don't disturb any clutches of eggs that you find
- Don't ride jet-skis or powerboats in the restricted zone of Laganas Bay

For more information see the National Marine Park of Zakinthos website at www.nmp-zak.org

Turtle nesting grounds

A 2km (1¼-mile) stretch of dunes and beach has been set aside as protected nesting grounds for the endangered loggerhead turtles which lay their eggs here each year. Nests are protected by wire enclosures and should not be disturbed (*see above*). *1km (⅔ mile) east of Laganas, stretching towards Kalamaki.*

Moni Anafonitria
(Anafonitria Monastery)

A survivor of several earthquakes, the monastery (it's also a nunnery) has a pretty medieval bell tower with faded frescoes, and a cell claimed to have been the refuge of Agios Dionissos, the island's patron saint.

40km (25 miles) northwest of Zakinthos Town. Open: daily, except during prayer.

Ormos Alikon (Alikes Bay)

This is the second-best swimming and sunbathing location on Zakinthos after Laganas, and those in search of less crowded beaches may rank it even higher as it is far less developed. It stretches for several kilometres – sandy at the southeast end, pebbly as the bay bends northwestwards. Two low-key resorts, Alikes and Alikanas, are separated by a 2km (1¹/₄-mile) stretch of yellow sand at the southeast end of the bay.

Approximately 15 to 20km (9–12 miles) northwest of Zakinthos Town.

Zakinthos Town (Zante Town)

The island's port and capital is a cheerful mixture of post-1953 buildings and a couple of medieval survivors, including a Venetian castle which stands on a hilltop 2km (1¹/₄ miles) from the modern town.

Northeast coast.

Agios Nikolaos

The lovely 15th-century church was restored after the 1953 earthquake and is one of the prettiest on the Ionian islands.

Platia Solomou. Open: daily.

A statue of the poet Dionysos Solomos stands outside the Museum of Neo-Byzantine Art

Kastro (Castle)

The mighty ramparts and turrets of the castle were strong enough to withstand not only the Turks but also earthquakes. It is one of the island's handful of surviving medieval buildings. On a clear day there is a good view of the mainland.

On the hilltop above Bohali village. Tel: (26950) 48099. Open: Tue–Sun 8am–2.30pm. Admission charge.

Museum of Neo-Byzantine Art

Works here include 15th- to 19th-century icons rescued from earthquake-demolished churches, and striking paintings from the 17th-century Ionian School. The artists of this movement, fleeing the Turkish conquest of Crete, combined traditional religious themes and Italian Renaissance influences in their painting.

Platia Solomou. Tel: (26950) 42714. Open: Tue–Sun 8.30am–3pm. Admission charge.

KITHIRA (Kythira)

Rugged and rocky, Kithira guards the western approaches to the Aegean from the Mediterranean (where the British fleet inflicted a decisive defeat on the Italian Navy during World War II). Traditionally, it is the seventh of the major islands of the Eptanisa, but is administered with the Saronic islands. In truth, it has little in common with either group, being separated from them by many kilometres of sea, and by the mountainous capes of the southern Peloponnese, while its fertile but mostly treeless landscapes and whitewashed villages look more like those of the Cyclades.

Steep sea cliffs surround much of the coastline, soaring up to a windswept plateau of thorn trees and deep ravines, studded with oasis-like patches of cultivated greenery. For much of its history, Kithira was plagued by pirates, and most of the upland villages (many of which are now almost deserted) are hidden from prevailing winds and unwelcome invaders in little sheltered valleys. Kithira has suffered even more than most Greek islands from emigration: by the end of the 19th century, more than 30,000 of its inhabitants had emigrated (almost all of them to Australia) and today its population stands at around only 4,000 people. So – except during July and August, when thousands of Greek-Australian emigrants return to visit their stay-at-home relatives – it is an excellent island for those looking for peace and quiet. Getting here is less challenging than it seems: there are regular domestic flights from Athens, even more frequent ferries from Githio and Neapoli on the southern mainland, and a weekly ferry connects the island (via its even more tiny and remote neighbour, Antikithira) with Kastelli on Crete. Kithira is bereft of great ruins from the ancient world, but if you are willing to explore (you will need a hired car or scooter to do so), the island's hinterland is dotted with evocative,

Kithira's castle offers magnificent views of the island

mostly ignored relics of the vanished worlds of Byzantium and Venice.

Hora (Kithira Town)

With its whitewashed houses and narrow, flagstoned, twisty streets, Hora owes more to the Cyclades than the Ionian islands. It consists of one main street, stretching along a steep-sided ridge, with houses spilling down into the steep gullies on either side, which are terraced into small fields and pastures with prickly-pear hedges.

This main street ends at the entrance to the prettiest little castle in all the Greek islands (as usual, known simply as Kastro – 'the Castle'). Within are the picturesque shells of the inner keep, a couple of small chapels, and half a dozen 18th-century iron cannon (three of which carry British insignia, for this little fortress was an outpost of British power for almost 50 years). The view from the castle is breathtaking. Close inshore is the huge, egg-shaped sea-rock which, according to ancient

Kapsali's two bays

Greek myth, is the egg from which the love-goddess Aphrodite hatched. You can just see Antikithira on the southern horizon, and a plaque set below the castle marks the birthplace of the Greek-American poet Lafcadio Hearn (1850–1904).

Hora overlooks the southern tip of the island. Entrance to the Kastro is free.

Kapsali

Immediately below Hora, Kapsali has beaches skirting two pocket-sized bays, both of which have clean water but slightly scruffy sand and pebbles. A string of tavernas and a row of pretty white houses with flower-filled gardens stretch around the harbourside, which until a few years ago was the main port of call for ferries connecting Kithira

with the mainland and Crete.
2km (1¼ miles) south of Hora.

Agia Pelagia

Ferries from Githio and Neapoli call at
this desolate harbour village set on a
narrow, gritty beach overlooked by
rocky hillsides. There is absolutely
nothing to keep you here, but because
Kithira has no public transport it is all
too easy to become stranded if you
disembark without your own transport.
If you plan to come to Kithira by ferry,
arrange for a taxi from Kapsali to
meet you at Agia Pelagia (ferry ticket
agencies in Githio and Neapoli can
do this for you). Failing that, helpful
islanders may be willing to offer you
a lift.
*Agia Pelagia is close to the northern tip
of the island, opposite Neapoli on the
mainland and 18km (11 miles) north
of Kapsali.*

Potamos

This workaday, crossroads village is the
largest settlement on the island, but
despite the presence of a couple of
quite charming small hotels it makes
fewer concessions to tourism than most
villages, being, sensibly, more involved
with the needs of local people than the
desires of visitors. Stay here if you really
want to see a slice of genuine island life
in the 21st century (billiards bar,
televised sport via satellite and Internet
café); otherwise, travel on to Hora or
Kapsali.
16km (10 miles) north of Hora.

Paleohora

The ruins of the Byzantine island capital
stand atop a crag with 100m (328ft)-high
cliffs on three sides. It was sited so that it
could not be seen from the sea, but this
did not save it from the feared Turkish
pirate Barbarossa, whose raiders sacked it
in 1537 (long after the fall of the
Byzantines, when the castle was taken by
the Venetians). It was never rebuilt, and
within its ruined ramparts are the walls
of an inner keep and the shells of several
dozen little churches and chapels built
during the Byzantine period.
*3km (2 miles) east of Potamos, 15km
(9 miles) north of Hora.*

Milopotamos

Hidden in one of the fertile ravines that
traverse the island's upland plateau,
Milopotamos is like a hidden, green
oasis, built around a burbling stream
which tumbles into a cool grotto. Its
waters are surrounded by local legend
and credited with healing powers.
6km (4 miles) north of Hora.

Spilea Agia Sofia
(Cave of the Holy Wisdom)

Byzantine frescoes can still be seen on
the inner walls of this chilly hillside
grotto, and there is good reason to
think that it may have been a sacred site
since the earliest times. Deep inside, the
250m (820ft) cave system is a fantasia
of limestone formations.
*3km (2 miles) from Milopotamos.
Open: May–Sept daily, 9am–1pm &
3–6pm.*

Cruise: Around Zakinthos

This cruise offers spectacular coastlines, a view of the island's less accessible beaches, and a glimpse of Zakinthos's mountainous northern neighbour, Kefalonia, on the horizon. Two or three boats leave Zakinthos harbour every morning in high season and tickets are sold by agencies at all the resorts, and by tour operator representatives.

The 60km (37-mile) round trip takes about 7 hours, including stops for lunch and swimming.

In early summer the sharp-eyed may be lucky enough to spot metre-long loggerhead turtles on their way to the egg-laying beaches (see p42), and there is always a chance of seeing dolphins, especially if the sea is particularly calm. Cold drinks are sold on board and lunch is usually included in the cruise price. Leaving Zakinthos harbour, the boat turns north, rounding the headland where the Venetian castle sits, then heads northwest along the line of the island's coast. Akr Tripiti (Cape Trypiti), the westernmost point of the Peloponnese mainland, can be seen on the eastern horizon.

1 Kastro (Castle of the Orsinis)

Above the harbour at Zakinthos stand the battlements of the medieval castle, built by the Orsini family, who ruled several Ionian islands in the Venetian era. That the castle survived the disastrous 1953 earthquake is testimony to the skill of its builders.

The boat cruises northwest, with the sands of Tsilivi beach on the port bow, and the hills and farmlands of northern Zakinthos above them.

2 Ormos Alikon (Alikes Bay)

Alikes Bay is a long sweep of sandy and pebbly shore, sheltering some of the finest beaches on Zakinthos at its southern end. Small resorts at either end of the bay are gradually linking up into one long strip of hotels and guesthouses.

Akr Skinari
Blue Caves ③
Korythi ○
Ormos Alikon
② Alikanas
④ Tsilivi
Anafonitria ○ Katastari
Zakinthos
Machairado ○ ① Kastro
Argassi
Kalamaki
Laganas ○ Vassilikos
Kolpos
Lagana Akr
Geraki
Keri ○
Akr
Marathia

N

○ ....Large Town
○ ....Small Town
★ ....Start of Cruise
○ ....POI
▬▬ ....Main Road

0   10km
0   5 miles

3 Blue Caves

The blue-water sea caves near the island's northernmost tip are Zakinthos's most striking natural attraction. A trick of the light makes the sea in and around the arched limestone caverns seem luminously blue. If you stop to snorkel you will find that underwater swimmers appear dyed blue too.

Rounding the northern promontory, the boat turns west. At this point, the 1,628m (5,341ft) peak of Mount Enos, the highest point on the Kefalonian coast, is clearly visible to the north.

4 Smuggler's Wreck

Stranded on a half-moon beach of rough, white sand, hemmed in by sheer limestone cliffs, is all that remains of the wreck of a Greek freighter which went aground in 1982, carrying an illicit cargo of cigarettes and liquor destined for Syria. Local tales say much of the cargo was never recovered.

The picturesque scene has been captured on a thousand postcards. *Most cruises stop at Smuggler's Wreck beach for lunch and for those who wish to swim, before returning to Zakinthos Town in the late afternoon.*

Cruise: Around Zakinthos

A perfect hideout – 'Smuggler's Wreck' beach

Argo-Saronic islands

Thousands of yachts, cruisers, ferries and freighters constantly criss-cross the waters of the Saronic Gulf (Saronikos Kilpos), between the peninsulas of Attica and the Argolid and the Isthmus of Corinth. The Gulf opens onto the Aegean to the south, with Pireas, the busy port of Athens, on its eastern shore. With the mainland so close, five of the six Saronic isles are attractive holiday spots, favoured by well-off Athenians, many of whom have second homes on Idra and Egina.

The ruin-studded shores of the Argolid peninsula divide the eastern Saronic Gulf from the western Argolic Gulf (Argolikos Kolpos), which bites deep into the Peloponnese mainland. The Argo-Saronic is home to four principal holiday islands – Egina (Aegina), Idra (Hydra), Poros and Spetses – plus the two lesser-known isles of Salamina (Salamis) and Angistri (Agistri), and many other unvisited rocks.

Only a hop away from Athens and its port of Pireas, these islands are a refuge for Greek city dwellers as well as holidaymakers. Many better-off Athenians have weekend homes here, and many more take advantage of the fast and frequent ferries and hydrofoils for a day's outing. Nevertheless, the islands are in many ways closer to the visitor's idea of a Greek idyll than many of those located in the Aegean's remoter reaches.

Salamina, the closest of the islands to Athens, is historically renowned, for it was in the straits between it and the mainland that Athenian triremes annihilated the Persian fleet in 480 BC. Nowadays, however,

it has virtually become an industrial and residential suburb of Athens.

There are few vehicles on these islands, and the little harbours with their steep tiers of white shipowners' mansions and villas are very much as first-time visitors to the Greek islands imagine them. They have avoided the kind of holiday invasion that has swamped less prosperous island communities.

Egina and its satellite Angistri, in the middle of the Saronic Gulf, are the closest of the group to Athens. Poros, further south, is only a few hundred metres off the Peloponnese coast. Idra lies midway between the Saronic and Argolic waters and Spetses is at the very tip of the Argolid peninsula.

Idra's picturesque harbour was once the base of wealthy sea traders

EGINA (Aegina)

The biggest of the Argo-Saronic isles, Egina has a fertile hinterland of little farms, a small fishing harbour where tiny boats unload even tinier whitebait, and one busy resort. During the War of Independence (1821–30), Egina Town was (for a time) the first capital of independent Greece.
25km (16 miles) south of Pireas.

Agia Marina

Egina's main resort, busiest at weekends and in Athens' mid-July to late August holiday season, is on a landlocked bay with a long, but usually crowded, sandy beach.
On the east coast.

Hora (Egina Town)

Egina Town's charm lies in its narrow lanes of pink and whitewashed houses, and its quayside cafés overlooking the old-fashioned fishing harbour and ferry port. It is an ideal spot for watching a typical Greek island port – chaotic activity when the ferry arrives, slumbering inactivity between sailings.
On the west coast of the island.

Kolona (Temple of Apollo)

A lofty, 8m (26ft)-high, fluted column marks the site of the 6th-century BC Temple of Apollo. Archaeologists have uncovered stretches of walls nearby from the same period. A museum displays finds from this and other excavations, including elegant fragments of sculpture.

THE ADMIRALS OF THE ARGO-SARONIC ISLANDS

When the War of Independence (1821–30) began, the wealthy admirals of Spetses and Idra turned their guns on Turkish targets. The Hydriot captains under Andreas Miaoulis (1769–1835) sent flotillas of fire ships packed with gunpowder which were sailed amid the Turkish fleet, then blown up. Spetses' most famous daughter, Lascarina Pinotzis (1771–1825), nicknamed Bouboulina, sailed at the head of her own squadron to raid Turkish harbours and convoys.

Immediately north of the town beach, about 750m (820yds) from the harbour. Tel: (22970) 22248. Open: Tue–Sun 8.30am–3pm. Admission charge.

Naos Afaia (Temple of Aphaia)

The loveliest and most complete of surviving Greek island temples. Built between 480 and 410 BC, 25 of its 32 tapering columns are still standing.
9km (6 miles) east of Egina Town. Tel: (22970) 32398. Open: daily 8am–7.30pm. Admission charge.

Paleohora

This derelict hillside village was Egina's capital until the 19th century and in its 18th-century heyday boasted around 400 houses and 20-odd churches and chapels. Some of these, from as early as the 13th century, have been restored. Venetian ramparts crown the hill above.
8km (5 miles) east of Egina Town, on the Agia Marina road.

ANGISTRI (Agkistri)

The tiniest of the main Saronic islands, Angistri has a single sandy beach at Skala, on its north coast. Crowded in the Athenian getaway season, it is quieter than the other isles for the rest of the year, and most of its islanders earn their livelihood through fishing and farming.

8km (5 miles) west of Egina.

POROS

Tiny Poros is so close to the mainland that you feel you could reach out and touch it – at its closest the Peloponnese is only 256m (840ft) away.

The island has but one village, also called Poros, and a scattering of shingle beaches. This harbour village is on the small peninsula of Sferia, facing the mainland. A narrow isthmus, which is known as Kalavria, connects Sferia to the hilly, pine-wooded main body of the island.

50km (31 miles) south of Pireas.

Askeli

Askeli is Poros's best beach, with fine, golden sand and crystal-clear waters, and has developed into a small but busy holiday resort.

About 3km (2 miles) east of Poros Town.

Moni Zoodohos Pigi (Monastery of the Source of Life)

This lovely whitewashed, cloistered building is dedicated to the Virgin, under one of her many Greek Orthodox guises as the Source of Life. The monastery stands in a grove of tall cypresses and has splendid views of the mainland coast. Below it, there is a pleasant small beach for swimming.

4km (2¹/2 miles) east of Poros Town. Tel: (22980) 22926. Open: daily 7.30am–12.30pm & 4.30–8.30pm. Admission charge.

Temple of Poseidon

The once great 6th-century BC temple has been reduced to a few stone walls

The Temple of Aphaia, one of the best examples of island temples

and is worth visiting more for the location than for what is left of the structure. In the 18th century it was used as a quarry for marble blocks for the building of a monastery on Idra.
8km (5 miles) northeast of Poros Town. Free admission.

Hora (Poros Town)

Cheerful and busy, Poros Town and its white boxy houses cover a beehive-shaped hillock, which is connected by a bridge and causeway to the main part of the island. The streets on and behind the lagoon-like harbour are cluttered with colourful stalls and shops.

Boats shuttle to and from the harbour, taking visitors to beaches around the island or across the strait to the mainland.
West coast, on Sferia peninsula.

SPETSES

The furthest of the Argo-Saronic isles from Athens, Spetses is just off the southern tip of the Argolid peninsula.
85km (53 miles) southwest of Pireas.

Spetses Town

Numerous 18th- and 19th-century shipowners' mansions are a feature of the island capital, which is a hideaway for the many well-off Athenians who keep second homes here, giving Spetses a much more stylish air.

The town is attractively laid out, with broad squares and avenues.
Northeast coast.

The hillside streets of Poros Town are home to colourful stalls and shops

Agios Nikolaos

The monastery of St Nicholas was the first building in the islands to fly the flag of independent Greece in 1821. Its courtyard is a mosaic of black and white pebbles in typically Spetsiot style.
On Palaio Limani (Old Harbour). Tel: (22980) 72423. Open: daily 8am–1pm & 5.30–9pm.

Moussio Laskarinas Bouboulinas (Laskarina Bouboulina Museum)

The home of Spetses' famous female privateer (*see p52*).
Signposted from Palaio Limani. Tel: (22980) 72416; www.bouboulinamuseum-spetses.gr. Open: late Mar–end Oct daily 9.45am–2.15pm & 3.45–8.15pm. Guided tours every 45 minutes.

Moussio Spetson (Hadjigiannis-Mexis Museum)

The former 18th-century home of Hadjigiannis Mexis, one of Spetses' wealthiest merchants, is now a museum dedicated to the great Spetsiot admirals of the 19th century, who played a leading role in the liberation struggle against the Turks.

Behind the Town Hall. Tel: (22980) 72944. Open: Tue–Sun 8am–3pm. Admission charge.

Many of the churches on the islands, often semi-derelict, are still in regular use

IDRA (Hydra)

Idra rides at anchor like a long, thin ship off the south coast of the Argolid peninsula. In the 18th century, at the height of its prosperity, Idra's merchant fleet numbered 160 ships, and 20,000 people lived here. The only vehicles on the island are two municipal trucks, and much of the island is covered by pines.

50km (31 miles) south of Pireas.

Idra Town

Idra charms new arrivals with a steep façade of tall stone mansions, white houses with pantiled roofs and a harbourside lined with chic cafés.

Midway along the north coast.

Kamini

Idra's most accessible beaches are pebbly strands at Kamini and Kastello.

1,000 to 1,500m (²/₃–1 mile) west of the harbour.

Mandraki

This is the only sandy beach on Idra and features a watersports centre.

3km (2 miles) east of the harbour.

Profitis Ilias and Agia Evpraxia

The monastery of Profitis Ilias and the nunnery of Agia Evpraxia are approximately two hours' steep walk from town, through pine forests that have just begun to cover the scars of the forest fire of 1985.

2km (1¼ miles) south of Idra Town. Tel: (22980) 52540. Open: daily, except during prayer.

Cyclades

There are almost 150 islands and islets in the Cyclades (Kiklades) archipelago, lying in a scattered circle in the southwest Aegean. Some are completely deserted, while others, such as Naxos and Paros, are comparatively large, fertile and populous. Mikonos and Santorini are the archetypal Greek islands – their blue-domed churches and white villages gracing thousands of postcards.

ANDROS

Close to the mainland, this large and prosperous island seems a little aloof from its southern sisters. Andros is a popular retreat for well-off Athenians, many of whom own holiday homes here. Perhaps because of this – and because it has no airport – there is little mass tourism here. But Andros is an attractive island, with a pleasant capital and decent beaches, and it's very easy to get to from the mainland port of Rafina, near Athens.

Hora (Andros Town)

The island's capital is a mixture of old and new, with a core of stately 19th-century merchants' mansions on a hilltop overlooking a harbour which is surrounded by more modern homes and buildings. There is a good, sandy beach (lined in summer with parasols and sunloungers) just south of the village, and another north of the harbour.

Moni Panahrantou (Panahrantos Monastery)

A few elderly and impressively bearded monks keep the Orthodox flame burning at this 10th-century fortified monastery which clings to grim grey and red cliffs and has sweeping views over the fields and olive groves below.
4km (2¹/₂ miles) southwest of Hora.
Tel: (22820) 51090. Open: daily sunrise to sunset.

Moussio Arkheologiko (Archaeological Museum)

The small archaeological museum is in the centre of town (signposted) and has a collection of finds from ancient sites on the island. The highlight of the collection is a 4th-century BC statue of Hermes.
Town centre. Tel: (22820) 23664.
Open: Tue–Sun 8.30am–3pm.
Admission charge.

Batsi

Andros's main beach resort has a long stretch of fine sand which draws the

Psara

Agiasmata   Marmaro

Volissos   Kardamila

Pelineo

Hios   Vrondados

Hios

Mesta   Kalimassia

Olimbi   TURKEY

Pirgi   Emborios

A e g e a n
S e a

Evia

Stira

Marmari

Karistos

Petalii

Andros

Gavrio   Hora

Batsi   Moni Panahrantou

Korissia

Otzias   Ormos
Panormos

Ioulis   Ormos Livadas   Gialiskari   Evdilos

Pisses   Kea   Tinos   Armenistis   Agios
Kirikos

Falatados

Akr Katakefalos   Siros   Hora   Panormos   Karkinagri   Ikaria

Loutra   Kithnos

Hora   Galissas   Ermoupoli   Hora   Mikonos

Merihas   Driopida   Finikas   Rinia   Platis Gialos

Kanala   Possidonia   Delos

C y c l a d e s

Serifos   Serifos   Naxos   Apolonas

Psili Ammos   Naoussa   Naxos   Donoussa

Megalo   Livadi   Parikia   Moutsouna   Donoussa

Livadi   Artemonas Kastro Antiparos Hora   Piso   Filoti

Kamares   Agios   Livadi

Apolonia   Georgios Aliki Paros Drios   Agiassos   Tholaria

Sifnos   Despotiko   Koufonissia   Pano Koufonissi   Krikelo 822

Kimolos   Platis   Iraklia   Egiali

Paleokastro Hora Gialos   Shinoussa   Katapola   Amorgos

Plaka   Psathi   Moni Zoodochou   Iraklia   Moni Hozoviotissa

Emborios Apolonia   Pigi   Gialos Ios   Kolofana   Hora

Adamas   Sikinos   Hora Milopotamos   Astipalia

Milos   Hora Sikinos Alopronia Manganari

Folegandros Karavostassis   Santorini   Hora

(Thira)

Thirassia   Ia

Thirassia   Thira Monolithos Anafi

Akrotiri Perissa   Hora Ag Nikolaos
Kamari

N

S e a   o f   C r e t e

○ ....Large Town
○ ....Small Town
■ ....POI
....Motorway
....Main Road
....Minor Road
✈ ....Airport
....International
Border

0   50km
0   30 miles

The hillside monastery of Panahrantos on Andros has wonderful views, but there are few monks to enjoy them

crowds from Athens in July and August (especially at weekends) but is less busy for the rest of the year. The beach is lined with modern restaurants, café-bars and small hotels.
12km (7 miles) west of Hora.

Gavrio

Nondescript Gavrio, close to the northwest tip of the island, is the main port for ferries and hydrofoils connecting Andros with the mainland and other islands in the Cyclades. It has a handful of places to eat and stay and a slightly scruffy beach, but it is really a place to pass through en route elsewhere rather than somewhere to linger.
18km (10½ miles) north of Hora.

TINOS

Tinos attracts hordes of Greek Orthodox pilgrims at Easter and on other holy occasions. In 1822 – at the height of Greece's struggle for national independence – a nun (later beatified as St Pelagia) dreamed of a 'miraculous' icon which was soon revealed on Tinos

and is now housed in the Church of the Annunciation in the centre of the island's main village. This quasi-sacred status (and a shortage of outstanding beaches) has preserved Tinos from the high-profile tourism that dominates its near neighbour, Mikonos, but it is an attractive spot for those seeking a peaceful holiday, with good walking on cobbled mule-paths that zigzag across its rolling hills, which are dotted with picturesque whitewashed and geometrically patterned dovecotes dating from Venetian times.

Hora (Tinos Town)

A pleasing clutter of unassuming 19th- and 20th-century houses rises from Tinos's harbour, dominated – at the upper end of a grandiose avenue built for pilgrims – by the imposing white marble Church of the Annunciation. The harbour is also remembered by many Greeks for the infamous sinking by an Italian submarine of the Greek cruiser *Elli* in 1940, before Italy formally declared war on Greece.

Panagia Evangelistria (Church of the Annunciation) and Tinos Archaeological Museum

This striking marble church looms over the village. Built in 1822, it guards the icon 'revealed' to St Pelagia, which is a symbol of Greek nationhood and is also believed by the credulous to have miraculous healing powers. On two key pilgrimage days, 25 March and 15 August, the church and the village are thronged by Orthodox believers. Also within the church complex is the archaeological museum, which displays a less than exciting collection of finds from sites on Tinos, notably an enormous 7th-century BC *pithoi* (earthenware storage jar).

Leoforos Megalohoris. Tel: (22830) 22670. Church open: daily 7am–8pm. Free admission. Museum open: Tue–Sun 8.30am–3pm. Admission charge.

MIKONOS (Mykonos)

Wealthy Greeks, stinking-rich expats and straightforward hedonists are drawn to this most iconic of Greek islands. The narrow streets of its labyrinthine main village are full of stylish jewellers and boutiques, its waterfront is lined with louche café-bars, and its nightlife is legendary. Equally legendary is the partying on the famous beaches, which are strung along the island's south coast, sheltered from the prevailing northerly winds which attract windsurfers to the wide bay of Panormos, on the island's north shore. Small boats and minibuses shuttle between Hora and the beaches from dawn till dusk in summer.

The nearby island of Delos can only be reached from Mikonos, and a visit to this most fascinating of ancient sites in the Cyclades is a must.

Ferries and cruise ships now dock at the purpose-built 'New Port' at Tourlos, 4km (2½ miles) north of Hora, leaving the old harbour clear for yachts, fishing boats and excursion cruisers.

Hora (Mikonos Town)

A row of derelict windmills overlooks the bustling crescent-shaped waterfront at Hora, where a crew of tame pelicans squabbles for titbits thrown from fishermen sorting their morning catch. On the south side of town, the Alefkandra waterfront (sometimes called 'Little Venice') is the most picturesque part of Hora, with the brightly painted wooden balconies of old town houses suspended over the sea and a plethora of stylish bars and restaurants.

Aegean Maritime Museum

Boat lovers of all ages will delight in this excellent collection of model ships, plans, maps and depictions of the vessels which have plied the Aegean from the legendary days of Jason and his Argonauts until recent times. The traditional sailing vessel *Evangelistria*, part of the museum collection, is moored in the old harbour in summer (June–September) and can be visited on the same ticket as the museum.

Next to Lena's House, at Tria Pigadia in the centre of Hora. Tel: (22890) 22700. Open: Apr–Oct daily 10.30am–1pm & 6.30–9pm. Admission charge.

Arxaiologiko Mouseio (Archaeological Museum)

The small but well-laid-out museum contains decorated vases and other finds from Classical-era sites on Delos and from the islet of Rinia. Pride of place goes to the Mikonos Pithos, a

Whitewashed walls and narrow alleys are typical of Mikonos

interior offers a glimpse of Mikonos in times gone by. Six rooms display antique furniture, icons, ceramics, prints and engravings.

Paraportiani, next to the church. Tel: (22890) 22591. Open: Mon–Sat 4.30–8.30pm. Admission charge.

Milos Boni (Boni Windmill Agricultural Museum)

The working windmill – one of a row of mills which overlook the harbour at Hora – is the centrepiece of a small outdoor museum which focuses on traditional island farming, with olive presses, a baker's oven, wine press and grain-threshing floor.

Leonidio Boni, Apono Mili, 300m (330yds) east of the harbour. Tel: (22890) 26246. Open Jun–Sept daily 4–8pm. Admission charge (same ticket as Folklore Museum).

Spiti Lena (Lena's House)

This annex of the Folklore Museum is a prettily preserved Hora town house, complete with its 19th-century fixtures and fittings, from plush divans and chairs to kitchen utensils.

Tria Pigadia, in the centre of Hora. Tel: (22890) 222390. Open Apr–Oct Mon–Sat 6.30–9.30pm. Admission charge (same ticket as Folklore Museum).

giant earthenware jar decorated with scenes of battling warriors from the Homeric sagas.

Andronikou (south end, signposted). Tel: (22890) 22325. Open: Tue–Sun 8.30am–3pm. Admission charge.

Laografiko Mouseio (Folklore Museum)

This 19th-century home with its traditionally decorated and furnished

Beaches

Mikonos's legendary beaches stretch in a chain along the island's south coast, and there is now precious little to differentiate them. All have fine sand but are so crammed with sunbeds that it is hard to tell, as well as watersports, and an array of summer café-bars and tavernas. Ornos, about 2km (3 miles) south of Hora, is the closest to town and the most family-friendly. Platis Gialos and Psarou are a little further east, sharing the same sheltered, south-facing bay but separated by a low headland, and are the most developed of the island's beaches. Still further east, about 8km (5 miles) from Hora, 'Paradise' beach (properly called Kalamopodi) and 'Super Paradise' (properly known as Plindiri) share a raunchy reputation for wild beach parties, round-the-clock dance music, and nude sunbathing.

PAROS

Loved by island-hoppers but somewhat ignored by package holidaymakers, Paros mixes Cycladic charm with rocking summer nightlife in the island capital, a handful of low-key man-made and natural attractions, and sandy beaches that rank among the best in the Cyclades. In ancient times, Paros was famous for its pure white marble, from which some of the greatest temples and artworks of the Greek world were carved. Three ancient marble quarry tunnels can be seen on the hillside at Latomia Marmaron, 6km (4 miles) east of the island capital, but the last marble deposits were worked out in the 19th century.

Parikia

Parikia is one of the busiest harbours in the Cyclades, with ferries calling constantly day and night, so it is an island-hopper's hub. Avoid cheap hotels on the 1.5km (1-mile) waterfront if you want a good night's sleep. The waterfront is lined with ticket agencies and scooter rental shops, café-bars and restaurants, with a bunch of late-night music bars and dance clubs at the southern end. A few blocks inland, however, Parikia becomes a much more peaceful labyrinth of narrow streets, whitewashed buildings, and quite stylish shops and bars. The remains of a miniature 13th-century Venetian fortress – built partly of column-stones from an ancient temple on the same site – stand not far from the town centre, on the north side of the harbour.

Archaeological Museum

This small but interesting collection includes pottery and marble fragments and a statue of Athena Nike dating from the 6th century BC.
Off Manto Mavrogenous, next to Panagia Ekatontapiliani. Tel: (22840) 21231. Open: Tue–Sun 8.30am–3pm.

Panagia Ekatontapiliani Byzantine Museum

Perched above the Parikia waterfront, this small church doesn't in fact have as many entrances as its name (which means 'hundred-gated') implies, but it is entered through a picturesque arcade

from which it gets its name. Parts of it date back to the 6th century, and its chapel incorporates columns from an even older Hellenistic temple. The south wing houses a small but spectacular collection of Byzantine religious artefacts, including richly embroidered robes, ecclesiastical crowns, and gilded shrines and censers.
Off Manto Mavrogenous. Tel: (22840) 21243. Open: daily 7am–11pm. Free admission.

Naoussa Bay

Naoussa, the island's second-largest settlement, stands on a fine, sheltered natural harbour on the north coast of Paros. Naoussa is still a working fishing village, but has gradually grown into the most stylish and upmarket resort on Paros, and has expanded westwards along a long, narrow crescent of sand, to almost join up with Kolimbithres on the opposite shore of the bay.
10km (6½ miles) northeast of Parikia.

Piso Livadi

On the east coast of the island, Piso Livadi is a cheap and cheerful cluster of purpose-built guesthouses, apartments and tavernas spreading out from a one-time fishing harbour. Some of Paros's

Naoussa is a cheerful blend of fishing village and holiday resort

poshest hotels are within easy reach, and the best beaches on the island stretch southward from the village, each separated from the next by a series of rocky headlands.

16km (10 miles) east of Parikia.

ANTIPAROS

Separated from its larger neighbour by a narrow channel, Antiparos is much quieter than Paros. Its single village (Hora) has plenty of small guesthouses and tavernas, a shuttle ferry connects it with Parikia (taking about 15 minutes) and its west coast has some superb and usually uncrowded sandy beaches, the best of which is at Agios Georgios.

Hora is 1km (²⁄₃ mile) southwest of Parikia; Agios Georgios is 12km (7 miles) south of Hora.

NAXOS

Naxos is the largest of the Cyclades and one of the most attractive islands in the group, with a fertile hinterland where olive groves, orange orchards, grain fields and vineyards cling to hillsides which rise to the central peaks of Zas (1,004m/3,284ft) and Fanari (908m/2,951ft) – the highest summits in the Cyclades. It has some fine beaches and a charming, busy little island capital that has not been overwhelmed by tourism, and remains almost undiscovered in comparison with its near neighbours, Paros and Mikonos. Naxos is roughly pear-shaped, measuring some 35km (22 miles) from north to south, and

most of its villages are on the western slopes of its central mountain ridge, while the steep, barren cliffs and rocky shores of the east coast are almost uninhabited.

Filoti (Naxos Town)

The island capital rises from a waterfront lined by modern buildings to an inner heart of Cycladic cottages and old Venetian town houses clustered around the walls and turrets of a 13th-century castle which was once the seat of the Sanudo dynasty. In 1207, in the aftermath of the infamous Fourth Crusade, the Venetian Marco Sanudo seized the island and his descendants ruled the Cyclades as Dukes of Naxos until they were ousted in 1566 by the corsair captain Khaireddin (also known as Barbarossa). The pretty little **kastro** (castle) is tucked away in a maze of alleys above the harbour. Restoration work on the castle is ongoing, and the Glezos Tower – the best-preserved part of the *kastro* – is being renovated by the National Archaeological Service, with plans to convert it into a museum of island heritage. Also within the *kastro* is the 13th-century cathedral, built during the reign of the first Sanudo Duke.

Naxos Archaeological Museum

An outstanding collection of ceramics and idols from the ancient Cycladic civilisation, well displayed and explained in an attractive 17th-century building which was once the island's main school.

Within the kastro. Tel: (22850) 22725.
Open: Tue–Sun 8.30am–3pm.
Admission charge.

AMORGOS

This slender, peaceful island is loved by those who have taken the trouble to

Gateway of the 6th-century BC Temple of Apollo

discover it. This is an island full of quirks, from culinary delights such as bright orange sea slugs and wild artichokes, to cliffside monasteries, ghost villages and – on a remote beach – a 'donkey graveyard', where donkeys too old to work were turned loose to die by their owners. Amorgos is the perfect stop on an imaginative island-hopping trip, with ferries heading south to Santorini and east to Astipalia and the Dodecanese.

25km (16 miles) southwest of Naxos.

Egiali

Once a sleepy, secondary port serving a handful of tiny villages in the far north of the island, Egiali has become the island's most popular holiday spot thanks to a vast sandy beach on a warm bay of shallow water, and now receives more frequent ferries than rival Katapola. Above its white houses and beach, several small villages perch on terraced hillsides above a delta of fertile farmland, overlooked by the bare 822m (2,697ft) peak of Krikelo.

In July and August, there's a surprisingly lively nightlife scene that starts around sundown at the cafés in the centre of the village, then moves on around midnight to the open-air music bars on the beach. For the rest of the summer tranquillity reigns. Egiali is the starting point for long hill walks that can take you through countryside dotted with abandoned villages, ending at the cliffside eyrie of the Hozoviotissa monastery.

MIGRANT BIRDS

Amorgos is on one of the main routes for migratory birds crossing the Aegean in spring and autumn, and autumn is an especially propitious time for birdwatchers. In October, flocks of hobbies swoop over the cliffs above Aiyiali, and squads of vultures and skeins of storks can be seen at high altitude as they head south to Africa.

10km (6 miles) east of Hora, on the northeast coast.

Katapola

Katapola, the port for the island's main village and the central and southern parts of Amorgos, is pleasant enough, with a row of tavernas and a few places to stay next to a horseshoe-shaped harbour that's popular with sailors, but most visitors quickly travel on to Hora and beyond.

Sub-aqua enthusiasts head for the far south of the island, where *The Big Blue* brought free-diving to the big screen more than 20 years ago. Incredible visibility and sheer walls vanishing into seemingly bottomless seas make Amorgos perfect free-diving territory, but for the less adventurous there are only a few fine sand-and-pebble beaches. *Katapola is 4km (2½ miles) below Hora, on the north coast.*

Hora (Amorgos Town)

The tumbledown shell of a modest little 13th-century castle built by the Venetian Ghisi dynasty overlooks Hora, the island capital. The village is a classic Cycladic gem, a citadel that comprises a clutter of narrow arched alleys where the blinding white stonework of old houses is brightened by green and blue woodwork, splashes of bougainvillea and pots of geraniums. Café tables fill a small, flagstoned central square, and the village streets have several art and craft shops selling better-than-average ceramics, prints, paintings and textiles.

Moni Hozoviotissa (Hozoviotissa Monastery)

The brilliant white walls of this emblematic 11th-century monastery cling miraculously to the bare cliff. Founded in 1088 by the Byzantine Emperor Alexios I Komnenos, its greatest treasure is an ostensibly miracle-working icon of the Virgin, kept in its own gold- and silver-lined chapel. *3km (2 miles) northeast of Hora, signposted. Tel: (22850) 71274. Open: daily 8am–1pm & 5–7pm. Admission charge.*

SANTORINI (Thira)

The view of Santorini from a ferry pulling into its cliff-ringed bay is unforgettable. Sheer cliffs in layers of red, white and greenish-grey volcanic rock encircle a huge, sea-filled caldera (crater) which plunges to an enormous depth and is encircled by the island and its smaller neighbours, Thirassia and Aspronesi. It also has two tiny, still-active volcanic islets that smoulder gently in the centre of the caldera.

(*Cont. on p68*)

Cruise: To Delos

In ancient times, Delos (Dilos) was a sacred and political centre and an important commercial port, and today its outstanding temple sites are among the most striking in Greece. The best way to visit them is by boat from Mikonos. Boats depart daily around 8.30–9am, returning from Delos at around 1pm.

The crossing takes approximately 30 minutes each way, leaving about 3 hours to explore the ruins.

Leaving Mikonos harbour, you have a view of the balconies of Alefkandhra ('Little Venice') overhanging the sea. The boat turns south, passing through the narrows between Delos and the neighbouring islet, Rinia, before arriving at Delos's harbour. There is a combined admission charge for site and museum. At the landward end of the pier, turn north and enter the sanctuary district via the Sacred Way, where the bases of the statues which lined this wide access path can be seen. After 100m (110yds) this leads to the three worn steps which are all that remains of the Propylaia, the great gate.

1 Hieron (Sanctuary of Apollo)

To the left of the Propylaia are traces of the 6th-century BC *stoa* (covered walk) of the Naxiots; on the right are the rectangular foundations of the 7th-century BC temple known as the House of the Naxiots.

The heart of the sanctuary comprises traces of three temples of Apollo, around which are the column bases and foundations of three smaller religious buildings.

A marble lion

Walk 400m (440yds) north, and leave the sanctuary via the walls of the 6th-century BC Temple of Leto, and the Agora of the Italians on your right.

2 Lion District

The row of five stone lions sculpted in marble from Naxos during the 7th–6th centuries BC are the best-known symbol of Delos. Originally there were many more. To the east is the site of the Sacred Lake (drained in 1924 to prevent malaria) where swans dedicated to Apollo once swam.

Turn right, around the site of the lake, and head back south 350m (383yds) to the museum, on your left.

3 Museum

The museum collection includes statues from the Sanctuary of Artemis, 5th-century BC Classical art, Hellenic sculptures and some delightful small bronze figures and ivory carvings.

Leaving the museum, continue south 500m (550yds) to the lower slopes of Mount Kinthos, Delos's highest point. Allow 45 minutes for ascent and descent.

4 Mount Kinthos (Oros Kinthos)

At the foot of the hill is the Terrace of the Foreign Gods, where once stood statues of Syrian and Egyptian deities.

After 200m (220yds), pass on your right the Sacred Cave, a cleft in the rock which was sacred to Herakles (Hercules) and had massive doors.

Descending Mount Kinthos, walk west 100m (110yds) to the 2nd-century BC Theatre District.

5 Theatre District

On your right, the courtyard of the House of the Dolphins features a superb floor mosaic of dolphins, which were sacred to Apollo. Opposite, the restored two-storey House of the Masks is one of the highlights of Delos, with more splendid mosaics. Finally, pass the well-preserved marble tiers of the Hellenic theatre, the House of the Trident, the House of Cleopatra (not connected with the famous Egyptian queen) and the beautiful panther mosaics of the House of Dionysos, before returning to the harbour.

Shaped like a broken circle, the island was formed by a huge volcanic explosion (*c.* 1450 BC) that blew out its centre, leaving the present huge caldera. Many archaeologists believe the explosion and the enormous tsunami it created may have been the nemesis of the Crete-based Minoan civilisation that collapsed at about the same time. (Minoan and Mycenaean sites have also been excavated on Santorini.) In more recent times, the island was also an important medieval possession of the Dukes of Naxos.

Santorini's main town, Thira, is a line of white battlements along the crater rim. South of it, the rolling hills rise a little further to the walls of Pirgos, a half-deserted fortress-village. To the east, the island shelves seaward in a series of terraced tomato fields and vineyards before reaching the sea at the black-sand beaches, Kamari and Perissa, on Santorini's east coast. A crescent ridge running from Pirgos to the east coast divides the island into two, and an ancient city (Akrotiri) once sat atop its seaward end.
50km (31 miles) south of Naxos.

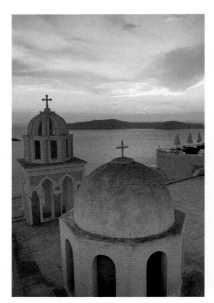
Firostefani church, Santorini

Akrotiri
(Akrotiri Archaeological Site)

The well-preserved houses and streets of this 'Greek Pompeii', smothered by the great eruption, have been excavated since 1935, unearthing graceful 3,500-year-old frescoes which demonstrate the connection with the Minoan civilisation. Some minor finds from the site are displayed in the Thira Archaeological Museum.
South coast of the southern cape, 18km (11 miles) south of Thira. Closed for technical works: no reopening date available at time of writing.

Kamari

Santorini's biggest resort is on a long, east-facing beach of black sand which becomes uncomfortably hot in the summer sun.
12km (7 miles) southeast of Thira.

Arkhea Thira (Ancient Thira)

Scant remains possibly dating from a 6th-century BC to 5th-century AD settlement include foundations of an ancient *agora* and a theatre.

On top of the Mesavouno headland, 2km (1¹/₄ miles) south of Kamari and 320m (1,050ft) above it. Open: Tue–Sat 8.30am–3pm. Admission charge.

Ia

This dazzlingly pretty clifftop village commands huge views, both across the northern and western horizon and south to Thira and Akrotiri. It was badly shaken by a minor eruption and tremors in 1956, and remained almost deserted until its restoration in the 1980s.

Many of its houses have typical Thira (Santorini) barrel-vaulted roofs (to withstand earth tremors), and some have rooms burrowed deep into the soft volcanic rock. A few have been converted into characterful guesthouses.

There is a small beach immediately below the village, reached by a steep stair cut into the rock.
8km (5 miles) north of Thira.

Thira

Thira's geometric buildings form a whitewashed parapet atop 270m (886ft)-high sea cliffs. Visitors arriving by sea reach the clifftop town either by donkey, up some 600 breathtaking steps, or by a dizzying cable-car ride from the harbour.

There are tiny blue-domed churches at every corner, but these are outnumbered by fast-food cafés and expensive jewellers. Thira is just too photogenic to have escaped mass-market tourism, and like Mikonos

(pp59–61) has been welcoming visitors since the early 1960s.

Arkheologiko Mousseo (Archaeological Museum)

A fine collection spanning two millennia, from the Minoan era to the Roman period.
Ipapantis St. Tel: (22860) 22217. Open: Tue–Sun 8.30am–3pm. Admission charge.

IOS

The Aegean's supreme party island throbs to a summer beat from June until September, when it attracts young ravers from all over the world who pack its bars, beaches and clubs. It is quieter in spring, early summer and autumn,

Ia, reborn as a holiday village

SANTORINI'S 'BURNT ISLANDS'

Two smouldering islets of volcanic rock, Nea Kameni and Palea Kameni, rise from the sea-filled caldera of Santorini. Palea Kameni has been there since the 2nd century BC, when it astonished locals by emerging from the sea in a few weeks. Nea Kameni, which rose from the depths between 1707 and 1711 and trebled in size in 1866–67, is still volcanically active, with a bubbling mud pool at its centre and hot-water springs rising through the sea around it. Both islets are the product of the same volcanic activity that blew Santorini apart around 1500 BC, leaving only the crescent-shaped island that we see today. Many archaeologists believe that a huge tsunami caused by that explosion wiped out the Minoan civilisation that dominated the Aegean world until that time, and which had its capital at Knossos on Crete, not far south of Santorini.

when it offers non-ravers a choice of fine sandy beaches. The island's sole claim to archaeological fame is the so-called 'Homer's Tomb' at Plakatos, 9km (5½ miles) northeast of Hora. Ios is one of many islands that claim a link with the author of the *Iliad* and the *Odyssey*, and the site – little more than a few tumbled gravestones dating back no further than the Byzantine era – is hard to get to and barely worth the effort.

Gialos

Every visitor's first sight of Ios is its harbour village, set on a fjord-like bay (Ormos Iou) with its own beach. Ferries call frequently en route to Pireas, Crete, Santorini, Naxos and other islands, and the harbour is ringed with cafés catering to those waiting for a boat. Shuttle buses connect Gialos with Hora, on the hilltop above the harbour.

1km (²/₃ mile) below Hora.

Hora (Ios Town)

Hora looks like most other Cycladic villages, with whitewashed stone houses set on narrow cobbled lanes, but moves to a modern beat. Almost every building is now a music bar, a café or a restaurant, and three generations of summer parties have virtually obliterated all traces of local culture.

Milopotamos

For most visitors this long, sandy, southwest-facing beach *is* Ios. Some people spend days or weeks here, sunbathing by day, partying into the small hours, then sleeping on the beach until sunrise. Milopotamos is a solid mass of sunbathing bodies by day, and boasts an array of bars, open-air dance venues, and watersports.

1km (²/₃ mile) from Hora.

Ormos Manganari

Small boats bring visitors from Gialos and Milopotamos to this chain of silvery sands overlooked by farmland on the south coast of the island. Though harder to get to, Manganari's beaches can be just as crowded as Milopotamos during the day, when a handful of small *cantinas* serve cold drinks and snacks to the masses.

12km (7 miles) southeast of Hora, access by boat.

Ormos Manganari on the island of Ios

SIKINOS

Tiny, rocky Sikinos is somewhat off the beaten track and is for Greek island purists. It has a hillside fortress-village, a ferry port with a small beach next to it, and a handful of other small beaches around its rugged coastline. With just a couple of very minor sights (both of them within walking distance of the main village) to attract the visitor's attention, this is very much an island for a quiet holiday lazing, swimming and reading.

Alopronia (Skala)

Inter-island ferries from Ios and Folegandros call at this small ferry port in a bay on the island's southeast coast. Alopronia also has a small beach and is popular with yachters, and there are a couple of small café-restaurants catering to those awaiting a ferry. It is also the base of the island's small squid-fishing fleet, which is busiest in early autumn – a great time to enjoy fresh-caught kalamari.
3.5km (2 miles) southeast of Hora.

Episkopi

Although it is also known locally as the 'Temple of Apollo', the true origins of this Hellenistic building, which became a Christian church in the 7th century AD, are forgotten. It may have been a temple or mausoleum and the exact date of its construction is unknown.

Hora (Sikinos Town)

Two hillside villages on the rocky spine of the island have merged into one cluster of whitewashed Cycladic buildings around a square of medieval houses which comprise the original medieval *kastro* (castle), along with a couple of tavernas.
3.5km (2 miles) from Alopronia.

Moni Zoodochou Pigi (Monastery of the Life-Giving Spring)

Climb to this now-deserted, tumbledown monastery for fine views over the slopes and valleys of Sikinos and across the channel to its western neighbour, Folegandros.
750m (820yds) above the kastro.

FOLEGANDROS

Tall and craggy, Folegandros looks like a stone ship steaming westward towards the mainland, with a scattering of tiny, uninhabited skerries in its wake. This island is one of the Cyclades' undiscovered gems, with a dazzlingly pretty main village which perches atop a dizzying cliff, offering fantastic views of neighbouring isles, including Santorini (Thira), Ios and Sikinos. Islanders claim that on a clear day you can see Crete, more than 100km (64 miles) to the south. Folegandros's hillsides are covered with small terraced fields where barley and olives thrive – testimony to centuries of hard peasant labour. The northeast coast is dominated by sheer cliffs, but there are some attractive small sandy beaches on the south coast, about 30 minutes' steep walking from the village.

Hora (Folegandros Town)

One of the loveliest Cycladic villages, Hora perches high above the sea among terraced hillsides, and is built around the *piatsa*, a stone-paved central square full of café tables shaded by mulberry trees. From the archway off the south side of the square, you enter a picturesque, dazzling-white, fortress-like warren of archways known as the *kastro* (castle). *In the centre of the island, 3km (2 miles) from Karavostassis.*

Karavostassis

Karavostassis (which literally means 'boat stop') is the island's tiny ferry port. There are a couple of small cafés close to the quayside, catering to those waiting for ferries, but there is no reason to linger here. Minibuses operated by several of the hotels and guesthouses in Hora meet most ferries. *Close to the southern tip of Folegandros.*

Hrisospilia

This sea-grotto filled with startlingly blue water whose Greek name means 'golden cave' bores into the cliffs of Folegandros's forbidding north coast. It can be reached only by sea, and small boats carry visitors from Karavostassis. *North coast, approximately 2km (1 1/2 miles) north of Karavostassis.*

MILOS

Milos's weirdly sculpted landscapes and coastline are the result of centuries of erosion of its soft volcanic terrain by wind and rain. The island's coasts are marked by twisted stone formations and offshore islands carved by the sea. The island has also been shaped by human effort: early Neolithic islanders valued the obsidian found here, and quarrying for cement and china clay continues today, so that some of the island's cratered landscapes – especially those of the Sarakiniko coastal plateau – look almost lunar. Milos is almost U-shaped, with a wide bay that takes a deep bite out of its north coast. Inland, it is surprisingly fertile, with splashes of pink oleander among terraced fields, and its hinterland is less mountainous than most of the Cyclades. Milos has a small airport with regular domestic flights to Athens and is also well served by ferries, but it receives surprisingly little tourism.

Adamas

Adamas, the island's pleasant, if prosaic, harbour town, sits on the north shore of the bay, which forms an excellent, sheltered natural harbour which in ancient times made Milos an important strategic asset for the fleets of Athens and its rival Aegean powers. Milos's defiance of Athens during the Peloponnesian War led to an infamous massacre when the Athenian authorities ordered their troops to kill the entire male population of the island.

Plaka (Milos Town)

The main island village, sitting on a hillside not far from its harbour, is a mixture of traditional and modern

The bizarre landscape of Milos

buildings on the site of an ancient city, the foundations of which can still be seen. The village has a number of small guesthouses and hotels, and a more than adequate choice of places to eat and drink. There are excellent views from the medieval *kastro*, a well-preserved Venetian citadel which stands on a hilltop about 500m (550yds) above the village, reached by a flight of cobbled steps.

Archaeological Museum and Ancient Milos

Traces of the ancient city include the remains of the 5th-century BC acropolis, an intact Roman theatre and 3rd-century AD Christian tombs. The Archaeological Museum contains Neolithic stone tools and earthenware, and a copy of the *Venus de Milo*, the famous statue of Aphrodite which was discovered on the seabed near Milos and is now in the Louvre museum in Paris.

500m (550yds) west/downhill from village centre. Tel: (22870) 21620. Museum & site open: Tue–Sun 8.30am–3pm. Admission charge for both.

Laografiko Mouseio (Folk Museum)

Costumes, furniture and decorative items from everyday island life in bygone days are exhibited in one of the grander old town houses in the centre of Plaka.

Village centre. Tel: (22870) 21292. Open: Tue–Sat 10am–2pm & 6.30–9.30pm. Admission charge.

Caves

The soft volcanic rock of Milos's coast has been hollowed out by the sea into a series of spectacular caverns which were used in the past by pirates and smugglers. At Kleftiko ('Robbers' Cave'), white chalk cliffs and pinnacles are honeycombed with caves. At Papafranga, three caves big enough to shelter large boats tunnel into the cliffside, and at Sikia ('Fig Tree Cave') a trick of the light makes the water appear to glow green.

On the southern coast of the island, all three caves are reached by boat from Adamas harbour, with several departures every week in summer.

SIFNOS

The island of Sifnos, rising steeply from the sea, is patchworked with fields and pastureland, criss-crossed with donkey-tracks marked out by drystone walls, and dotted with white hill villages.

136km (85 miles) south of Pireas.

Apollonia (Hora)

Three characterful hamlets – Artemonas, Kamares and Katavati, originally about 750m (820yds) from each other – have blended into a single jumble of whitewashed houses, church towers and small, café-cluttered squares.

Centre of the island.

Agios Spiredon
(Church of St Spiridon)

The island's main church, built and added to over several centuries, is a fine example of the Sifniot taste for multi-coloured religious architecture, painted in gaudy shades.

On Stylianou Prokhou, the village's main street.

Laografiko Moussio
(Folk Museum)

Beautiful island lace and embroidery, displays of traditional Sifniot costume, and a rusting collection of lethal weaponry.

On the central square at Kamares. Tel: (22840) 33730. Open: daily 10am–2pm & 7.30–11.30pm. Admission charge.

Kastro (Castle)

This medieval Venetian stronghold occupies the finest natural fortress on Sifnos, a sea-crag guarded on three sides. Its distinct alleys, archways and two-storey houses suggest a strong Venetian flavour.

East coast, 4km (2¹/₂ miles) east of Apollonia.

Archaeological Museum

Small collection of finds from the ancient site.

Pano Kastro. 3km (2 miles) east of Apollonia, on the coast. Tel: (22840) 31022. Open: Tue–Sun 8.30am–3pm. Admission charge.

Moni Chrysopigi
(Chrissopiyi Monastery)

This picturesque 17th-century monastery, located on a promontory on

the east coast, is one of the island's tourism symbols. It is deconsecrated, and you can stay in one of the monks' cells in summer.
6km (4 miles) southeast of Apolonia. Tel: (22840) 71295. Open: sunrise to sunset.

SERIFOS

Serifos is how many people picture all the Greek islands. White houses, churches and a miniature castle all cling precariously to a crag some 2km (1¹/4 miles) inland from a perfect natural harbour on a shallow sandy bay. Around the bay, square houses splashed with purple and scarlet flowers clutter the hillside, where clumps of greenery cling to the scree and boulder-strewn slopes of rocky ravines.
131km (81 miles) southeast of Pireas.

Livadi

Serifos's port is a cheerful, house-proud assortment of mostly modern, well-kept homes, tavernas and small hotels, enhanced by its bayside location and mountain backdrop. A tiny fertile delta of green farmland and pink oleander-lined creeks stretches behind the village. The tree-lined beach south of the village is not the island's best: there are much better, small sandy beaches 10 to 30 minutes' walk away, beyond the headland west of the harbour.
2km (1¹/4 miles) southeast of Serifos Town.

Megalo Livadi

This west-facing beach is the remotest and least-visited large beach.
8km (5 miles) southwest of Serifos Town.

Moni Taxiarchon (Monastery of the Archangel Michael)

The 16th-century monastery is often deserted, with a single guardian monk sporadically in residence. There are some minor frescoes within, but the visit is worth making as much for the walk through serene hill landscapes as for the destination.
2km (1¹/4 miles) northwest of Kallistos village, 5km (3 miles) north of Serifos Town. Access on foot from Kallistos.
(*Cont. on p78*)

White houses cling to the hills on Serifos

Cruise: Santorini crater

This cruise gives superb views of the fantastically coloured volcanic cliffs of Santorini (Thira), with the white villages of Santorini and Ia clinging to the rim of the giant sea-filled crater – the most striking island landscape in the Aegean. Tickets for the trip are sold by tour agencies in Santorini and Kamari, and at the larger resort hotels (if you are on a package tour they can be booked through your tour representative).

Boats depart from Skala Thiras, at the foot of the west-coast cliffs directly below Thira. Most departures are at 9 or 9.30am, returning mid-afternoon.

1 Donkey ride

A cobbled, zigzag staircase descends for 270m (886ft) from just below Thira to the small pier at Skala Thiras. You will have to haggle furiously over the price if the donkey ride is not included in the price of your excursion. Of course, you could simply walk down, but it's a long, hot descent and the steady donkey traffic makes it even less enjoyable, as the donkey drivers show little consideration for pedestrians.

2 Crater wall

Leaving Skala Thiras, look back for a magnificent view of the multicoloured cliffs, banded with shades of red, pink, white and green volcanic rock. Fragments of porous pumice stone can be seen floating in the bay.

After 15 to 20 minutes, land at Nea Kameni, 2km (1¼ miles) west of Athinios.

3 Nea Kameni

The eerie, lifeless island of shattered black rock is the product of a series of volcanic eruptions (*see p70*). Hot springs and boiling mud trickle from cracks in the rock and a smell of sulphur hangs over the islet. Just south and west of Nea Kameni is the smaller Palaia Kameni, also formed by volcanic activity, which first appeared in the 2nd century BC.
The boat sails round Nea Kameni's north coast, heading west towards Thirassia. Look south for a view of Santorini's dramatic southern cape, Akrotiri, where archaeologists have unearthed remains of a Minoan settlement almost 3,500 years old (see p68).

4 Thirassia

Thirassia is a tinier reflection of Santorini. Its cliffs are all that remain of the original island, shattered by a titanic explosion 3,500 years ago. As on

Santorini, the main village – also called Hora – is reached by steep steps from the harbour below. Pause here to enjoy the view across the crater. Hora has several small, scenically located tavernas which will allow you to do just that while enjoying a cold drink.

Walk west and downhill across the island (30–45 minutes each way) to a choice of small, pebbly and sandy coves on its western coast, where you can swim and sunbathe; or take the less energetic option, and swim from the tiny pier below Hora, where the deep blue water is extremely clear and shoals of colourful fish make for excellent snorkelling.

5 Ia

On the return boat trip, look north to the clifftop village of Ia, perched on the extreme tip of Santorini. It was shaken badly by tremors in 1956, but is now restored to pristine whiteness. Below the village at sea level, you can see the mouths of tunnels carved into the soft volcanic rock, used by the islanders as homes, stables and boathouses.

6 Cable-car ascent

From Skala Thiras, take the dizzying cable-car ride from sea level to the cable-car station for a final view of Thirassia and the crater islands.

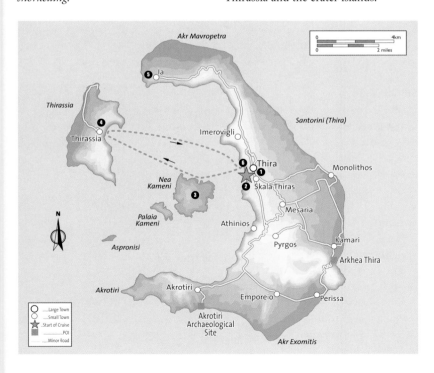

Sketchily signposted. Open: irregular hours. Enquire at Serifos Town community office or at Kallistos.

Psili Ammos

Serifos's best beach, with a lovely crescent of white sand facing east.
4km (2¹/₂ miles) north of Livadi. Access on foot or by boat.

Serifos Town (Hora)

Serifos Town is built around and within the walls of a Venetian castle, which is virtually absorbed into the buildings around it. Unlike some horas, therefore, it does not stand in splendid isolation, but is just another part of the pleasant jumble of old stones and whitewashed walls.
2km (1¹/₄ miles) from the east coast.

SIROS (Syros)

One of the most populous islands, with 20,000 inhabitants, Siros is fertile on its west side, barren on its eastern coast, and blessed with the southern Aegean's finest deep-water anchorage.
40km (25 miles) northwest of Naxos.

Ermoupoli

Ermoupoli, Siros's capital, is no dinky village but a thriving town of 15,000 people. Its grandiose town architecture and neoclassical public buildings date from the first half of the 19th century, when it was newly independent Greece's most prosperous city. It wasn't until the completion of the Corinth Canal in 1893 that it was eclipsed by Pireas, the port of Athens.

The lower part of the town, between the harbour and main square, Platia Miaoulis, was laid out in the island's heyday. Above it, on two hills, Ano Siros to the west and Vrondado to the east, are the town's contrasting medieval quarters. Ano Siros is a labyrinthine collection of alleys and arches with a scattering of Catholic churches dating from the Venetian era, while Vrondado is the town's Orthodox quarter.

Agios Georgios (Cathedral of St George)

The Roman Catholic cathedral is built in the Venetian style.
On top of Ano Siros, 1km (²/₃ mile) from Platea Miaoulis. Tel: (22810) 88809. Open: daily. Free admission.

Grandiose buildings overlook the busy harbour at Ermoupoli

Anastasi

The grand, domed Orthodox church was built to rival the nearby Catholic cathedral, Agios Georgios.

At top of Vrondado, 1km (2⁄3 mile) north of Platea Miaoulis. Tel: (22810) 82998. Open: irregular hours. Enquire at town tourist office, Platea Vardhaka.

Archaeological Museum

Finds from Siros and nearby islands.

West side of the town hall, signposted. Tel: (22810) 88487. Open: Tue–Sun 8.30am–3pm. Admission charge.

Mone Kapoutsino
(Capuchin Monastery of St John)

Built in 1535, the monastery survived the Turkish era under French protection.

100m (110yds) downhill from Agios Georgios.

Finikas/Possidonia

Siros's main beach resort, where two villages, at either end of a pebble-and-sand bay which faces west, have merged.

11km (7 miles) southwest of Ermoupoli.

KEA (Tzia)

Kea is only an hour from the mainland by ferry, with frequent services from Lavrion (20km/12 miles away, on the east coast of Attica), so it is popular with Athenians, many of whom have holiday homes on the island. As a result, it is both very Greek and surprisingly cosmopolitan, but sees very few foreign visitors, and outside the peak Greek holiday period of July to mid-August it can be very peaceful. It is an excellent island for walkers, with more than 36km (24 miles) of walking paths, many of which are ancient cobbled mule-tracks, and all of which are clearly waymarked. Kea also has numerous small pebbly beaches and an attractive island capital.

Ioulis (Kea Town)

The island's main village overlooks a pretty wooded valley and is a mix of traditional homes with red-tiled roofs and wrought-iron balconies, and more modern buildings, most of which have happily been designed in keeping with existing island architecture. A tumbledown Venetian castle, built partly with marble blocks from an ancient sanctuary of Apollo, stands about 1km (2⁄3 mile) from the centre of the village and is clearly signposted, as is the island's most famous sight, the Lion of Kea, a 3m (10ft)-high effigy of a lion, carved into the rock of a hillside 2km (1 1⁄4 miles) from the village during the 6th century BC.

Archaeological Museum

In the centre of the village, the museum has a fine collection of artefacts from the sites of the four cities which shared the island in ancient times, including parts of the Temple of Athena at Karthea.

Platia Mouseio. Tel: (22880) 22079. Open: Tue–Sun 8.30am–3pm. Admission charge.

Crete

Mountainous, dramatic and alluring, Crete (Kriti) is Greece's biggest island – almost 260km (160 miles) long from east to west, but not much more than 70km (35 miles) from north to south at its widest point. Three impressive mountain ranges form its spine, with peaks that overlook more fertile lowlands on the north coast and beaches and coves lapped by the Libyan Sea on the south side of the island.

Most of the millions who come to Crete every summer stay in the large resorts that sprawl along the north coast, from Sitia in the east to Hania in the west. Iraklio (Heraklion), the island capital, is an ever-growing sprawl of modern buildings around a historic inner core. Not far east of the capital and its airport, there's an almost continuous string of resorts which merge into each other from Hersonissos as far east as Malia. By contrast, the Elounda peninsula, still further east, is home to some of the most luxurious self-contained luxury hotels in the Mediterranean, replete with opulent suites, villas and bungalows, manicured grounds, private beaches, tennis courts, spas and gourmet restaurants.

On the south coast, there are smaller-scale resort developments in and around Plakias, Agia Galini, Matala and Makrigialos. Except in July and August, this part of the island is less crowded

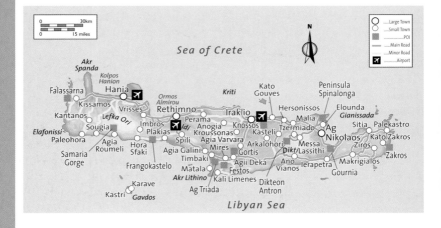

than the bustling north, and much more attractive for the independent traveller hoping to get away from the crowds.

Crete's mountain ranges are high enough to be snow-capped in winter, and patches of snow last until May on the highest peaks. Traversed by dramatic gorges, mule-tracks and way-marked walking trails, Crete is one of the most attractive – and challenging – islands for walkers.

But its landscapes also have a gentler side, with remote hill villages tucked away on wooded slopes, oasis-like hidden valleys, olive groves and lush orange and lemon plantations, and plentiful vineyards that produce some of Greece's best wines.

Crete is the southernmost of the Greek islands. Spring comes early, in a blaze of wild flowers, and summer lingers on until at least the end of October, making it the perfect isle for an early- or late-season visit.

Island-hoppers can combine a visit to Crete with a journey through the Cyclades, as there are frequent ferries connecting Iraklio with Santorini and points north. You can also head east to Rhodes and the Dodecanese by sea or air.

Crete's history is as rich and varied as its geography. From the late 3rd millennium BC it was the seat of Europe's first civilisation, the Minoan empire, which from its capital at Knossos dominated the Aegean. After the collapse of the empire in around 1500 BC, Crete's importance faded until the Roman conquest of Greece. The Romans left some impressive monuments, but as Rome's power diminished the island was ravaged by pirates and Saracen invaders. In AD 961 the Byzantine emperor Nikiforas Fokas drove the Saracens out, but in 1204 it was seized from Byzantium by a new rival power, Venice. The Venetians dominated the island until 1669, when they in turn were driven out by the Turks. Nevertheless, it is Venice that has left the most indelible mark on the island, with massive Venetian fortifications overlooking the harbours and enclosing the historic centres of Crete's major towns.

Iraklio (Heraklion)

The island capital is more appealing than it appears at first sight, with an inner core of historic streets partly surrounded by 17th-century Venetian ramparts which are easiest to see at Porta Hanion (Hania Gate). Iraklio's ancient harbour is overlooked by a Venetian fortress, the Koulos, and the great stone archways of the Arsenali, the shipyard used to build and maintain Venice's fleet of war-galleys and trading ships.

Iraklio is a busy commercial town and the island's major seaport, with ferries and cargo ships constantly arriving and departing. It also has some super, authentically Greek cafés and restaurants. Also well worth a morning visit is the old market area along Odos 1866, where traders sell everything from traditional Cretan daggers to bunches of herbs, leather

A 16th-century Venetian fortress guards the harbour at Iraklio

centre). Tel: (28102) 231940. Open: daily 8am–7.30pm. Closed: public holidays. Admission charge.

Archaeological Museum

Here you can see the most remarkable finds from Knossos, as well as relics from other, later Hellenic and Roman sites on Crete.

Halidhon Street, signposted. 100m (110yds) from the harbour. Closed for renovation; scheduled to reopen in 2012. Some key exhibits on display in temporary exhibition next door.

Agios Nikolaos

This charming little harbour town surrounds a small fishing port and a picturesque inner lagoon lined with tavernas. It is a pleasant place for a quiet holiday, and a good base for exploring the eastern part of the island.

Rethimno (Rethimnon)

The lanes and cobbled market streets of this old Venetian harbour town are overlooked by a massive fortress, the late 16th-century Fortetsa (or Frourio), built by the Venetians and extended by the Turks. The older part of town is a charming mix of Turkish and Venetian influences and there are some excellent restaurants and a choice of charming small hotels. West of the harbour, larger and more modern hotels stretch along a palm-lined esplanade behind a long, sandy beach.

95km (59 miles) west of Iraklio.

goods, and even buckets of live snails (a local delicacy).

Knossos

The capital of the ancient Minoan empire, rediscovered by a British archaeologist in the early 20th century, is the most imaginatively reconstructed ancient site in Greece, with colourful painted columns supporting the roofs of massive halls and lining broad avenues.

5km (3 miles) southeast of Iraklio (bus 2 from city bus terminal on Epimenidou, or a 10-minute taxi ride from the

Archaeological Museum

The most interesting facet of this museum is its collection of coins from almost every era of Crete's history.

Off Melissinou, opposite the southwest corner of the Fortetsa. Tel: (28310) 29975. Open: Tue–Sun 8.30am–3pm. Admission charge.

Hania (Chania)

This pretty, old-fashioned town with its pastel-coloured, neoclassical mansions grouped around a twin harbour overlooked by Venetian walls bubbles with fun during the summer, with a lively after-dark scene centring on bars and cafés along the harbour promenade until around midnight, when the party moves on to seaside bars and clubs just outside town. Hania has an excellent small archaeological museum, a great covered market and an old-fashioned bazaar just inland of the harbour.

Archaeological Museum

Mysterious Minoan relics, Hellenic marble statuary and elegant Roman pottery and jewellery are on display in this excellent small museum.

Halidon, signposted (about 100m/110yds inland from harbour). Tel: (28210) 90334. Open: Tue–Sun 8.30am–3pm. Admission charge.

Festos (Phaistos)

It takes a powerful imagination to make much of the hilltop remains of this Minoan palace dating from *c.* 2200–1700 BC as there is little to be seen

besides underground chambers and foundations. Nevertheless, there are breathtaking views of the mountains and the Libyan Sea.

56km (35 miles) southwest of Iraklio. Tel: (28920) 42315. Open: Tue–Sun 8.30am–3pm. Admission charge.

Gortis (Gortyna)

Much less ancient than nearby Festos (it dates from Roman times), Gortis is, however, much more impressive, with the splendid ruins of a Hellenic-Roman city, temple foundations, the remains of an *agora* (marketplace) and an early Christian basilica.

44km (27 miles) south of Iraklio. Tel: (28920) 31144.

Lassithi

The fertile Plain of Windmills, ringed by totally bare mountains high on the Dikti massif, is a much-touted day-trip destination. The drive from the coast on winding mountain roads is spectacular.

61km (38 miles) southeast of Iraklio.

Dikteon Antron (Psychro or Dikti Cave)

The Lassithi region's main attraction is this green, mossy, 250m (820ft)-deep cavern full of twisted stalagmites, where Zeus, greatest of the Greek gods, was born – or so legend has it.

1km (²/₃ mile) above Psihro village, signposted. Steep path, practical shoes and torch essential for cave. Tel: (28340) 31207. Open: Apr–Oct daily 8am–7pm; Nov–Mar Tue–Sun 8.30am–3pm. Admission charge.

Walk: Samaria Gorge

This challenging but very rewarding walk takes you through the most impressive mountain scenery in the Greek islands, from the top of the longest mountain gorge in Europe to the lovely pebble beach at Agia Roumeli. The gorge is a national park, so camping, swimming in the freshwater pools and straying from the marked track are prohibited. It is open from May to mid-October, depending on rainfall.

Allow 4 to 6 hours for this strenuous 18km (11-mile) walk.

Start from Omalos village, 36km (22 miles) south of Hania. The head of the gorge is signposted Xiloskalo. On leaving the village, you will receive a numbered ticket (no admission charge) that you surrender at the other end.

1 Xiloskalo (Wooden Stair)

The wooden steps, made of solid logs, start at 1,227m (4,026ft) above sea level and drop steeply into the bottom of the gorge, turning into a footpath which descends almost 1,000m (3,281ft) along a 2km (1¼-mile) stretch.

2 Gingilos

Above you on your right, as you start the descent, is the towering flank of Mount Gingilos, climbing to a sharp peak almost 1,000m (3,281ft) above Omalos.

After the steep descent, the path becomes less tiring and zigzags down grassy slopes, amid pine woods, with springs gurgling in the rocky stream bed.

3 Agios Nikolaos

The tiny, whitewashed chapel of Agios Nikolaos, with candles always burning in front of its icons, stands in a small pine wood to the right of the path.

1½–2 hours' walking from Agios Nikolaos, through pine forest and across the stream bed, will bring you to the deserted village of Samaria.

4 Samaria

This ghost village, with its derelict stone cottages and abandoned mill and olive press, has been deserted for half a century. One house is used as the park warden's office. Samaria is the midway point of the walk, and there is an official picnic area under the pines where you can take a break.

From Samaria, the path passes another small chapel, Osia Marias, then winds along the stream bed, crossing it several times by chains of water-smoothed boulders. The gorge narrows like a funnel, with the slopes on either side becoming steeper until you reach the narrowest point.

5 Sideresportes (Iron Gates)

The gorge is narrowest at this point. Grey cliff walls, marked with the rust-coloured stains of iron-bearing springs, shoot vertically to 600m (1,969ft). High above, the sky is a narrow strip of blue. Water surging through the narrows makes the gorge impassable in winter and early spring, and even in summer you may have to take off your shoes and paddle across the stream.

From Sideresportes the gorge fans out into a boulder-filled delta, and the cliff walls recede to become steep, rocky slopes, wooded in places. Walking is fairly easy for the final 5km (3 miles) to the sea at Agia Roumeli.

6 Agia Roumeli

This tiny village exists only to service the steady flow of summer walkers. A chain of tavernas and small guesthouses extends the length of a pebbly beach ending in cliffs to the west but extending several kilometres eastward. The water is very clear and a swim is welcome.

Independent travellers can opt to stay overnight at Agia Roumeli before walking on eastward to Hora Sfakion (where the road from Hania ends), or to travel on east or west by boat. Those on organised tours will be transferred by boat to Hora Sfakion to meet their coach.

Xiloskalo, the wooden stair, drops steeply into the Samaria Gorge

Walk: Samaria Gorge

Dodecanese

The Dodecanese (Dodekanissa) island group contains something for everyone, with an array of landscapes ranging from the farmlands of Rhodes and Kos to the stark hillsides of Kalimnos and the smouldering volcanic crater of Nissiros. There are big, bright beach resorts, miniature havens that see only one ferry a week, mosques and monasteries, ancient temples and medieval castles.

The chain of islands runs close to the Turkish coast in Greece's southeast Aegean, and the name 'Dodekanissa' means 'twelve islands' – but the Dodecanese also includes an assortment of tiny isles whose people are numbered only in hundreds or even in dozens. These include Megisti, Greece's easternmost outpost, within a few hundred metres of Turkey; Saria; Pserimos; and the mini-archipelago of Lipsi (Leipsoi), Arki (Arkoi) and Agathonisi, east of Patmos.

Some of these, such as Pserimos and Lipsi, are close to popular holiday islands and are regularly invaded by flocks of day-trippers. Others, such as Agathonisi or Arki, attract only the most determined of island-hoppers.

With frequent ferry and hydrofoil connections between the major islands and to Pireas and other island groups north and west, the Dodecanese group is perfect for island-hopping.

Man-made sights include the grand walled city of Rhodes, restored to its medieval splendour, the fortified monastery of St John on Patmos, and the ruins of classical Hellenic and Roman cities on the islands of Kos and Rhodes.

Dodecanese houses have a distinctive style of their own, typified by tall two- and three-storey homes with neoclassical stucco façades in pastel shades, tall doors and shuttered windows. Many have wooden or wrought-iron balconies, and most have gardens or courtyards overflowing with vines, pelargoniums and often banana and palm trees. You will also see Art Deco public buildings, erected during the Italian occupation (1912–43).

The climate is mellower than that of the windswept islands of the central Aegean. The Dodecanese are spared the gusty *meltemi* (dry north wind) which sometimes plagues the Cyclades, and Rhodes claims more hours of sunshine per year than anywhere else in Europe, making it the only truly year-round holiday destination in the Greek islands.

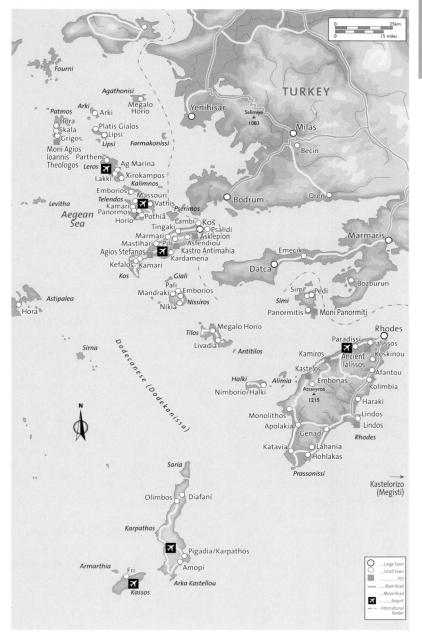

Dodecanese

KOS

Kos, the third largest of the Dodecanese, is a long, fish-shaped island of changing landscapes. The higher slopes of Mount Dikios (Oros Dikeos), which dominates the northeast of the island, are rugged and treeless, while its lower slopes are clad with pine and fig trees.

Northwestern Kos is covered by wheat fields and cattle pasture. Inland, much of the island is a plateau of meadows, thorn trees and goat pastures. The southern tip is mountainous, but its shores are studded with small beaches.

There are excellent beaches all over Kos, and the island is a favourite holiday destination for northern Europeans.

Like Rhodes, Kos was a stronghold of the Knights of St John, who left behind two formidable castles. Turkish and Italian occupiers also left their mark.

In 1933, the island was struck by an earthquake which levelled much of Kos Town, allowing the Italian authorities to excavate archaeological sites that had been built over.

Midway up the chain of the Dodecanese, Kos has excellent connections by ferry and hydrofoil to its neighbours, and westwards to the Cyclades and Athens, making it a popular island-hopping junction.

Kalimnos, Pserimos and Nissiros are all close enough to be popular day-trip destinations, as is Bodrum in Turkey.
110km (68 miles) northwest of Rhodes.

Kardamena

Kos's biggest and busiest resort features long, southeast-facing beaches to either side of a small fishing harbour, surrounded by a long strip of bars, discos, hotels and restaurants. Until the late 1970s, it was no more than a village. Today it could be anywhere in Greece. The conical silhouette of the isle of Nissiros (*see pp91 & 94–5*) can be seen on the southern horizon, and excursion boats arrive daily from Kardamena harbour in summer.
25km (16 miles) southwest of Kos Town.

Kastro Antimahia

The impressive angular battlements surrounding the hilltop date from the mid-14th century. The Knights of St John rebuilt the castle in the 15th century, and the crest of Grand Master del Caretto is carved above the main gate (which itself is within a much later Italian gun-casement). The small chapel of Agia Paraskevi within the ramparts dates from 1494.
18km (11 miles) southwest of Kos Town, 4km (2 1/2 miles) northeast of Kardamena. Free admission.

Kefalos

Kefalos is a small, relaxed resort overlooking one of the island's best beaches, the long, south-facing strip of Kamari. It is the best place on Kos for a quieter holiday, avoiding the crowds and the frenzied nightlife of Kardamena. There are other beaches to the north and south, reached on foot

over hill paths, or by small boats which operate frequently throughout the summer.
45km (28 miles) southwest of Kos Town.

Agios Stefanos (Basilica of St Stephen)

Ruins comprising the walls and columns of a 5th-century Christian basilica.
North end of Kamari Bay, next to the Club Med resort. Free admission.

Palatia (Ancient Kos)

A 4th-century BC sanctuary of Demeter and the tiered seats of an ancient theatre have been excavated at the site of the island's first city. In 366 BC, the capital of the island was moved to the site of modern Kos Town.
2km (1¹/₄ miles) southeast of Kefalos. Free admission.

Kos Town

The modern capital is an agreeable blend of Greek and Roman ruins, medieval fortifications, Turkish leftovers and florid Italian public buildings. Visitors can mingle with the everyday bustle around the crescent harbour and the busy market area, where high-piled produce stalls, gaudy souvenir stores and smart goldsmiths' shops stand next to each other.
East end of the island.

Agora

The site of the *agora* (a marketplace), dating from the 4th century BC, contains foundations of several temples, sections of the town walls, a Christian basilica and the extensive foundations of the Roman city of Kos.
Access from Platia Eleftherias, signposted. Tel: (22420) 28326. Open: daily. Admission charge.

Dodecanese

Kardamena beach, Kos

Dodecanese

Palm trees and bougainvillea brighten the ruins of Neratzia Castle

Archaeological Museum

The main exhibits are the 4th-century BC statue of Hippokrates and a mosaic of Asklipios (*see below*). Other finds span the 3rd century BC to the 2nd century AD.

Platia Eleftherias. Tel: (22420) 28326. Open: Apr–Oct Tue–Sun 8.30am–8pm. Admission charge.

Asklepion

This is one of the best-preserved and most beautifully located sacred places in the Aegean islands. Seven white Corinthian columns of a 2nd-century AD Roman temple have been re-erected, and the arched walls of the terrace have been rebuilt. Two columns of the 4th-century BC Temple of Asklipios (god of healing) can also be seen.

4km (2¹/₂ miles) southwest of town centre, signposted. Tel: (22420) 28326. Open: Tue–Sun 8.30am–8pm. Admission charge.

Casa Romana

A reconstruction of a 3rd-century AD Roman villa with mosaics, three inner courtyards and baths.

Grigoriou tou Pemptou. Tel: (22420) 28326. Open: Tue–Sun 8am–2.30pm. Admission charge.

Kastro Neratzia (Neratzia Castle)

The medieval Knights' castle, a low square of sloping ramparts and turreted bastions that stands guard over the harbour.

South side of harbour. Open: Tue–Sun 8.30am–7.30pm. Admission charge.

Odeion

The *odeion* (Roman theatre) has 14 tiers of marble seats. Opposite, on the other side of Grigoriou tou Pemptou, is a second extensive archaeological site, covered with a confusing clutter of marble capitals and fallen columns.
West end of Grigoriou tou Pemptou.
Tel: (22420) 28326. Open: Apr–Oct daily 8.30am–8pm. Admission charge.

Marmari

Kos's west coast is an almost continuous strip of sandy beaches, but prevailing strong winds make them less popular among holidaymakers than the more sheltered strands of the southeast. There are exceptions, and Marmari is one of them. Windsurfers rate it among the best in Europe for its steady breezes.
Southwest coast, 15km (9 miles) southwest of Kos Town.

Mastihari

An unassuming port with a small beach, Mastihari's main attraction is the ferries which leave regularly for Kalimnos and the little island of Pserimos. Southwest of Mastihari, the coast is windswept and unappealing.
West coast, 30km (19 miles) southwest of Kos Town.

Pili

The ruined ghost village of old Pili on the southwest shoulder of Oros Dikeos (Mount Dikeos) is appealing in a tumbledown way. Hidden in a wooded glen, it is dominated by the shell of a Byzantine tower. Half a dozen small chapels indicate that the village was quite prosperous in its medieval heyday, when its inhabitants huddled below the protecting castle to escape marauders from the sea. Unfortunately, their wall paintings are not well preserved.
1km (²/₃ mile) southeast of modern Pili, 23km (14 miles) southwest of Kos Town.

Tingaki

The best beach close to Kos Town. Tingaki is sandy, but like all the west-coast beaches it can be blustery.
12km (7 miles) west of Kos Town.

Zia

Zia is the most visited and the prettiest of the Mount Dikeos villages. By night, tour coaches arrive for typical 'Greek evenings' in recently built tavernas. Come here in the daytime for the fine mountain scenery and the views of the island and its northern neighbours.
12km (7 miles) southwest of Kos Town.

NISSIROS

The tiny southern neighbour of Kos is blessed with a charm out of all proportion to its size. Its mountainous coast encircles a vast inner hollow, in the centre of which are several volcanic craters. By contrast, picturesque white villages cling to the seaward side of the slopes, looking out over thick forests.

(*Cont. on p94*)

Walk: Kos Old Town

One of the charms of the island capital is the clutter of medieval and ancient sites painstakingly uncovered after the 1933 earthquake. This easy walk takes in the highlights of the oldest part of the city (see pp88–91), including relics which span several millennia of Kos' fascinating history, from Roman times through to the era of the Knights of St John and the Ottoman empire.

Allow 2 hours.

Start from the south side of the harbour, beneath the castle, whose ramparts are the town's most obvious landmark.

1 Kastro (Castle of the Knights of St John)

Inner and outer ramparts were built between 1450 and 1478 using many blocks looted from ancient temples. Impregnable towers at each corner strengthen the mighty defences, and with this castle and its twin at Halikarnassos (modern Bodrum, Turkey) the Knights controlled the strait between Kos and the mainland. *Leave the castle by the wooden footbridge, crossing the dry moat to reach Platia Tou Platanou, the small square leading to the first archaeological site.*

2 Platia Tou Platanou (Hippocrates' Tree)

The giant plane tree, its great boughs spreading to shade the entire square, clings stubbornly to life although its trunk is completely hollow and its branches are supported by scaffolding. To have shaded Hippocrates, it would have to be more than 2,400 years old, making it the oldest tree in Europe. *Cross the square to enter the first of the Old Town's two archaeological sites.*

3 Agora Archaeological Site

This was the site of the Roman town and it was strikingly designed with a flight of broad steps connecting it with the harbour. The street plan, including foundations of temples and civic buildings and paving from ancient streets, can be clearly seen. Nearby are the foundations of the *agora* (marketplace), including the toppled columns and bases of several temples. *Leave the site by the Platia Eleftherias gate. The Archaeological Museum is on the north side of the square, signposted.*

4 Archaeological Museum

A collection of Roman and Hellenic sculpture depicts Hippocrates, Hygieia (goddess of health) and Hermes (messenger of the gods), while a mosaic of Hippocrates and Asklipios (the god of healing) decorates the courtyard.

5 Defterdar Mosque

The dome and minaret of the Defterdar Mosque, built in the 18th century, stand above Platia Eleftherias on its south side. The arcaded ground floor is now occupied by small shops.
Leave Platia Eleftherias by the west side, turning on to the pedestrianised Odos Ifestou.

6 Odos Ifestou (Bazaar)

Originally the heart of the medieval Turkish bazaar area, the modern pedestrianised street is mainly taken up by souvenir stores and jewellery boutiques. Reminders of the Turkish era include a fountain with Koranic inscription (where Ifestou meets Venizelou) and a minaret close to the west end of Ifestou.
At the west end of Ifestou, cross Platia Dhiagoras to enter the town's second archaeological site.

7 Odeion and Archaeological Site

The lively mosaics and wall paintings uncovered in the ruins of 3rd-century AD Roman houses are the main attraction of this site. Other highlights are the pillars of the gymnasium and the beautifully restored Nymphaion, which dates from the 4th century BC.

With its mosaics, well and statues, it was first thought to be a sanctuary to all the goddesses. Only later was it discovered to be a public urinal.

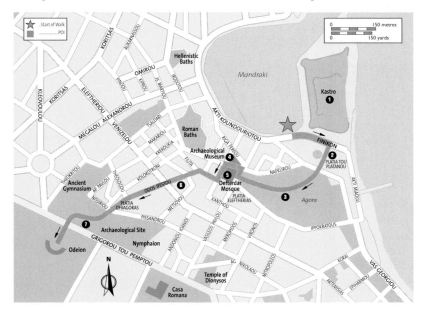

The island's volcanic soil is extremely fertile, and this, together with earnings from the cement quarries on the islet of Giali, has given Nissiros a degree of peaceful prosperity.

Seen from a distance, the thick bush clinging to its slopes makes the island look almost tropical, though its beaches don't live up to this first impression, comprising pebbles and brownish sand. As a result, Nissiros sees few tourists apart from excursionists from Kos, who make a flying visit to the crater before heading back, and it still feels pleasantly remote from 'civilisation'.
12km (7 miles) south of Kos.

Emborios

This almost deserted village has spectacular views out to sea and the Kos coast. For equally awesome views down into the old crater with its patchwork of fields, follow the

Blue-painted balconies in Mandraki's main street

whitewashed steps to the highest point of the village, where there is a pretty hilltop church in good repair.
6km (4 miles) east of Mandraki.

Stefanos Crater

Around the crater, the hillsides are streaked with sulphur, and the air smells like the aftermath of a fireworks display. The crater itself is a bowl 250m (820ft) wide and 30m (98ft) deep. Fumaroles emit steam from deep underground, and grey mud, stained by brimstone-yellow sulphur deposits, heaves and bubbles. Here at the bottom, the ground temperature can reach 120°C (248°F).
Centre of the island.

Mandraki

Most of the island's 900 or so inhabitants live here in the main village, a network of narrow lanes and squares rising uphill from the esplanade, where fish tavernas sit by the sea wall. These look north to Kos and the strange silhouette of the quarry island Giali. The harbour, where ferries and excursion boats from Kos dock, is about 750m (820yds) east of the village.
Northwest corner of the island.

Paleokastro

Grim ramparts of spectacular black volcanic rock guard the island's oldest defensive site. It has been fortified throughout the ages, from the Dorian era (2,600 years ago) to the days of the Venetians and the Knights of St John.

The brilliant white village of Emborios on Nissiros perches above the crater

1km (²/₃ mile) south of the village, signposted. Free admission.

Panagia Spiliani (Church of the Virgin of the Cave)

Built into the mountain, within battlements erected by the Knights of St John, this monastery church dates from 1600 and has a valuable iconostasis.
Overlooking the village, signposted. Open: daily 7.30am–3pm & 6–8.30pm. Admission charge.

Nikia

This spectacularly located village makes a dazzling splash of white against the rugged mountainscape of the crater rim.
10km (6 miles) southeast of Mandraki.

Moni Agios Ioannis Theologos (Monastery of St John the Divine)

A whitewashed monastery church, perched precariously on the upper slopes, looking down into the crater.
500m (550yds) below Nikia, on the

signposted path to the crater. Not usually open.

Pali

This little fishing village has a large harbour where traditional wooden fishing boats are built and yachts anchor, plus an esplanade lined with tamarisk trees. To the east, its long brownish sandy beach is the most easily accessible on Nissiros.
3km (2 miles) east of Mandraki.

KALIMNOS

Kalimnos is an island of deep blue, fjord-like bays and striking bare white limestone hills, pockmarked with caves and dotted with green valley deltas of cultivation where the mountains meet the sea.

With so little fertile land, islanders have (until the advent of tourism) been dependent on the sea, and Kalimnos's sponge-divers ventured as far as the North African coast, Florida and even Cuba. These days, the sponges which

The arms of the Knights of St John on the castle at Horio

are sold everywhere on the island are more likely to have been imported (many, ironically, from Florida) than to have been hauled up by local divers.
15km (9 miles) north of Kos.

Horio

Horio is Kalimnos's medieval capital, built inland for protection from pirate raids. It is now a residential hillside suburb of Pothia, with many dignified old homes in tree-filled gardens.
3km (2 miles) northwest of Pothia.

Kastro (Castle)

This small, crumbling castle is Byzantine, more than 1,000 years old, with Venetian additions dating from the 13th century. The heraldic arms of the Knights of St John are carved above the gateway.
200m (220yds) above the village. Free admission.

Emborios

From its pebbly beach, this tiny fishing hamlet (just waking up to the

possibilities of tourism) seems to be entirely landlocked, with steep hillsides rising to surround a deep, calm, crystal-clear inlet which offers fine swimming and snorkelling.
16km (10 miles) northwest of Pothia.

Massouri and Mirties

These two fishing hamlets lie at either end of a stretch of beach on a bay which is sheltered by the long, thin islet of Telendos. They have grown into a pleasant small resort strip of small hotels, pensions and restaurants. The beaches are a mix of pebbles and sand and the water is calm and very clear.
8–9km (5–5^1/$_2$ miles) northwest of Pothia.

Pothia

Prosperous from the 19th-century sponge trade, Pothia is a charmingly cluttered harbour surrounded by dolls'-house-like mansions and cafés, patronised by elderly traders and captains in panama hats or seamen's caps, many of them retired from sponge-fishing in Florida or the Bahamas.

Pothia's town hall (midway along the harbourfront) is a fine example of the 'Art Deco Moorish' style invented by the Italians for their public buildings in the Dodecanese, with elaborate domes, arches, round windows and plaster mouldings.

Archaeological Museum and Vouvalis Mansion Museum

This great little archaeological museum covers a much greater span of Greece's past than many bigger rivals. Draped in bronze, the 'Lady of Kalymnos' faces the entrance to the stylish new wing, which houses archaic finds from the island's caves, classical bronzes, statuary and ceramics.

Next door is the Vouvalis Mansion annex where the lifestyle of a 19th-century trading dynasty (whose sponge-diving empire stretched from the Aegean to North Africa, the Caribbean and Florida) is preserved in all its maroon plush and gilt-mirrored glory.

Enoria Aghias Triadas/Plateia Kyprou. Tel: 22430 23113. Open: Tue–Sun 8.30am–3pm. Admission charge.

Vathis

This is the miniature port of the farming settlement of Vathis. It is an enchanting ex-pirates' lair, where a narrow arm of the sea, only barely wide enough to allow fishing boats or yachts to pass, widens into an inner lagoon. The cliffs shelter the inlet and the village, and radiate the sun's heat in summer, even after sundown. Swim from the steps at the end of the pier, which lead into deep, clean water.

6km (4 miles) northeast of Pothia.

Telendos

Telendos, Kalimnos's tiny and mountainous satellite, shelters the waters off Mirties and Massouri, and has beaches and a little hamlet of its own. There are regular small boats

from Mirties that run throughout the day in summer.

1km (²/₃ mile) west of Mirties.

LEROS

Leros is a peaceful island that sees far fewer visitors than its neighbours to the north and south. Its beaches, if not breathtaking, are certainly uncrowded, and its harbour towns, if not over-endowed with purpose-built tourist attractions and facilities, are undeniable slices of authentic Greek island life.

There is also a fertile hinterland of rolling hills, terraced fields and olive groves, which is ideal if you like undemanding rambles in a rural setting. This is one island where the locals still outnumber the visitors all year round.

Barren hills rise behind Pothia, the sleepy harbour capital of Kalimnos

Platanos Castle looms over Leros

Leros's coastline is deeply indented, making it look like a piece from a jigsaw puzzle, and though it is only 17km (11 miles) from its northern to its southern tip it has more than 70km (43 miles) of coastline. The superb anchorage at Lakki, on the west coast, made the island a strategic prize in World War II. The events on which the book and film *The Guns of Navarone* are loosely based took place here in 1943 when, following the Italian capitulation, British troops attempted to occupy the island before it could be secured by Germany, only to be expelled by a stronger and better-supported German force. The islanders and their homes suffered severely in the fierce fighting.

Agia Marina (Platanos)

Agia Marina, Leros's eastern port, is really three villages which have merged into one higgledy-piggledy town spanning a hilly, castle-topped headland with harbours on either side. Agia Marina surrounds the main northern harbour; Pandeli lies on a smaller fishing harbour; Platanos, below the castle on the headland, separates Pandeli and Agia Marina. *East coast.*

Kastro (Platanos Castle)

The first castle on this site was built by the Byzantines, but the tower and ramparts that now crown the village were strengthened by the Venetians and the Knights of St John and are again being restored. The castle is still garrisoned by the Greek army, as its location, with panoramic views over many kilometres, makes it a perfect lookout point.

Within the castle is a small museum exhibiting pottery and other finds from excavations around the island, and a small monastery church, Panagia (Church of the Virgin). No monks live here any more, but there is a reputedly miraculous icon of the Virgin.

Immediately above the centre of Platanos, signposted from Platanos. Open: sunrise–sunset. Free admission. Photography forbidden. Church open: irregular hours.

Alinda

The best beach on the island and its only developed resort, Alinda has a narrow, shingly beach, and attractive views across the bay to the castle at Agia Marina (Platanos), Leros's only historic sight.

4km (2^1/$_2$ miles) northwest of Agia Marina.

Lakki

Lakki, on one of the finest natural harbours in the Aegean, has recovered from near ghost-town status to become the island's main ferry harbour and commercial centre, with an array of shops, tavernas, bars and places to stay. During the Italian occupation (1912–43) it was a major naval base, and the Italians bequeathed a number of opulent-looking Art-Deco buildings and wide palm-lined boulevards.

West coast, 4km (2^1/$_2$ miles) south of Agia Marina.

Xirokampos

The northern coast of the neighbouring isle of Kalimnos, not far south of Lakki, appears almost to fit into the narrow bay of Xirokampos, where a small farming village sits among fields and palm trees behind a long, narrow beach.

10km (6 miles) south of Agia Marina.

PATMOS

Patmos is an island of great natural and man-made beauty, crowned by the ramparts of an impressive medieval monastery and by the most striking village in the Dodecanese.

On the coast, lovely blue bays almost cut Patmos in two and there are lots of secluded little beaches. Inland, low rocky hills are covered with terraced fields, divided by a maze of drystone walls topped with thorns. Ranks of eucalyptus trees, a late introduction, shade island streets, and fig trees, bougainvillea and prickly pear cluster around houses and villages.

The fact that Patmos has been proclaimed a holy island, maintains monastic conservatism and has no airport has helped to keep tourism quite low-key, though the legendary monastery does make this one of the better-known islands in the Dodecanese.

60km (37 miles) northwest of Kos.

Grigos

Patmos's most accessible beach lies in a steep-sided east-coast bay. The setting is hard to beat, though the beach is pebbly and no better than average.
5km (3 miles) south of Skala.

Hora (Patmos Town)

Patmos' capital is one of the most beautiful in Greece, well worth the steep walk up from Skala. Tall mansions in grey stone and white plaster date from its 17th-century heyday, when islanders owned a substantial merchant fleet. Around them are simpler village homes. The colours are austere, an almost monochrome mix of white walls and grey stone doorways and arches, and it is almost impossible to keep a sense of direction in these corridor-like lanes, stairs and passages. Patmos Town – like many old Greek villages – is much bigger than it appears at first sight. To find your way out of the maze, just keep heading downhill.
1–2km (^{2}/$_3$–1^1/$_4$ miles) above Skala.

Moni Agios Ioannis Theologos (Monastery of St John the Divine)

The grand monastery around which Patmos Town is built is the island's claim to fame. Founded in the 11th century, it was self-governing under the Byzantine emperors and kept its independence when the Venetian Dukes of Naxos acquired Patmos in the 13th century. Its grim black battlements and bastions make it look more like a fortress than a place of worship. They were built to protect the treasures of the monastery from pirate raids and were added to throughout the Middle Ages, with the great sloping buttresses dating from the 16th century.

Inside the walls is a central courtyard lined with domed arcades and paved with a mosaic of black pebbles. The Katholikon (main church) of the monastery stands to the left of this courtyard. Built in 1090, its interior is decorated with 17th-century frescoes of the life of St John. The chapel of the Virgin in the main church has remarkable late 12th-century frescoes, uncovered and restored in 1958.

Next to the Katholikon is the monastery museum, which has a gorgeous collection of icons, holy vestments and church furniture.
Centre of the village, signposted. Tel: (22470) 31234. Open: May–Aug Sun 8am–1pm & 2–6pm, Mon & Thur–Sat 8am–1.30pm, Tue–Wed 8am–1.30pm & 2–6pm.

Skala

The island's main village and harbour is on a perfect anchorage, which makes it a popular port of call for yachts. It is a verdant, flower-filled village, and its handful of medium-sized hotels are unobtrusive among the more traditional whitewashed buildings. The harbourside is lined with café tables which, after dark, attract a more stylish clientele than you would expect on this remote little island, many of them Athenians and

Deep blue bays, almost cutting Patmos in two, make Skala a perfect anchorage

foreigners who own homes in Patmos Town.

The grand black battlements of the Monastery of St John frown down on Skala from their hilltop site.
East coast.

ASTIPALEA

Geographically and culturally one of the Cyclades, Astipalea was lumped with the Dodecanese islands by an accident of history. When international arbitrators were brokering the independence of Greece from Turkey (1832), they drew the line west of the island, and it remained under foreign rule until 1947.

The island is barren and rocky, almost cut into two by deep bays. The isthmus between them is just wide enough for the road to pass. Though remote, Astipalea is popular with fashionable Athenians and its only

village, Astipalea Town, is surprisingly stylish.

Hora (Astipalea Town)

The chic island capital is striking even by Cycladic standards. Its white houses, with two or three storeys and pretty painted shutters, combine influences from its western sisters and from the islands further east. They cover the hilltop above a perfect natural harbour.
Northwest Astipalea.

Kastro (Castle)

The dilapidated Venetian-Turkish castle has an endearingly slapdash appearance. Its walls are cobbled together from slabs and blocks looted from earlier buildings. It enjoys panoramic views to the empty horizons around the island.
On the highest point of the village.
Free admission.

KARPATHOS

Karpathos is a lonely island. Long sea crossings separate it from its nearest large neighbours, Crete in the southwest and Rhodes in the northeast. Rugged and mountainous, it has excellent beaches and attractive villages. A charter airport ensures that, despite its remoteness by sea, it gets its share of tourism, but as Karpathos is the second largest of the Dodecanese (after Rhodes), it absorbs its summer visitors without becoming overcrowded.

An island of changing landscapes, its fertile southern half is connected to the more barren and mountainous north by a knife-edged mountain ridge which in places is just wide enough to carry the road. Bus rides can be vertigo-inducing. In the north is one of the island's highest peaks, Profitis Ilias, reaching 1,140m (3,740ft).

Like many islands, Karpathos lost many of its people to emigration in the 19th and early 20th centuries, most of them heading for the eastern United States, which is why you may meet older men, retired to their island birthplace, speaking fluent English with Brooklyn and New Jersey accents. Many family homes have been colourfully rebuilt with money earned overseas. Local tastes run to vivid blue and green plasterwork, domes and archways, offset by purple and crimson bougainvillea.

Though Karpathos shares some of the history of its Dodecanese neighbours to the east, with occupation by Byzantines, Venetians, Knights of St John and Turks, none of them left much in the way of tangible remains, but the island compensates for that by offering walkers the finest rambles in the Dodecanese, whether in the gentler valleys and vineyards of the south, or in the breathtaking mountain landscapes of the north.

60km (37 miles) southwest of Rhodes.

Amopi

Karpathos's growing holiday resort has a choice of three sandy beaches and an increasing number of hotels and tourist tavernas.

8km (5 miles) south of Pigadia (Karpathos Town).

Olimbos

The principal village in northern Karpathos, Olimbos is awesomely situated on a high, windy ridge which plunges sheer to the west coast of the island. A line of stone windmills stands along the ridge, some of them still in use. Above the village is Profitis Ilias, one of the island's highest points. Olimbos was one of the most isolated villages in the Aegean until the building of the road from Pigadia in 1980. Its small port, Diafani, 3km (2 miles) away on the east coast, is too small for inter-island ferries to dock. As a result, it retains much of the old-fashioned self-sufficiency and many of its traditions.

40km (25 miles) north of Pigadia.

Pigadia (Karpathos Town)

The capital is a well-kept, unassuming modern harbour where boats call en route from Rhodes to Crete. Its redeeming feature is its proximity to the fine, 2km (1¼-mile) sandy beach of Ormos Vrondis, which begins immediately north of the town's harbour.

On the southeast coast.

Vroukounda (Vrychonta)

These scattered ruins of various eras include the foundations of a small temple, a Byzantine-Turkish keep, rock graves and a shrine to Ayios Ioannis Theologos (St John the Divine) in a cliff cave.

North of Pigadia. Free admission.

KASSOS

This southernmost island of the Dodecanese group is a delight for island purists. Here tourism has had zero impact. There is nothing to do except ramble among tiny fields and olive groves, sit in cafés, and swim and sunbathe.

10km (6 miles) south of Karpathos.

Fri

The island capital is ringed by mountains and set on a rocky bay, enlivened only by infrequent ferries from Crete and Karpathos. Its dignified older homes belong to shipowning families whose fleets brought prosperity in the 19th century, and its port, Emborios, is a 10-minute walk away.

A line of dilapidated windmills stands on the ridge above Olimbos on Karpathos

The Knights of St John

Founded to succour wounded Crusaders and pilgrims in the Holy Land, the Knights of St John were expelled from Palestine after the fall of Acre in 1291, and settled on Cyprus until they transferred to Rhodes in 1309. Seizing the Dodecanese as well as the port of Bodrum on the Turkish coast, they built new castles or strengthened existing fortifications on almost all the islands. They also built a city of palaces and lodges – one for each of the 'tongues' of the order –

St Paul's Gate leads into Rhodes Old Town, fortified by the Knights of St John

within the great ramparts of Rhodes Old Town.

Each 'tongue' represented one of the eight different lands – Aragon, Auvergne, Castile, England, France, Germany, Italy and Provence – whose lodges and crests you can see on Odos Ippoton, the restored Street of the Knights in the old town of Rhodes.

There were never more than 650 Knights of the order in total, though with their wealth they commanded a fighting force of much greater numbers.

The Knights ruled the seas of the eastern Aegean for the next two centuries, and though they claimed to be defenders of Christendom, their galleys preyed on any vessels they could catch, including those of Greek islanders and merchants. In 1522, however, Suleiman the Magnificent attacked Rhodes with a huge fleet and a 100,000-strong army. Only 200 Knights survived the six-month siege, finally withdrawing after a negotiated surrender. As they were vastly outnumbered, it was a tribute to their fighting prowess and to the strength of their defences that they held out so long. The huge stone cannonballs fired by the Turkish siege guns can still be seen littering the dry moat around the old quarter.

The Knights later moved to Malta, granted to them in 1530 by the Holy

Palace of the Grand Masters of the Knights

Roman Emperor Charles V. Though their piratical ways did not endear them to their Greek neighbours, Mussolini decided that they were suitably militant role models for Fascist Italy, and under the Italian occupation of Rhodes the battlemented Palace of the Grand Masters, the lodges of the eight 'tongues' and other relics of the Knights were painstakingly restored, which explains why they are in such good repair compared with most other medieval buildings in the Greek islands.

Rhodes

The biggest and most important island of the Dodecanese chain, Rhodes (Rodos) has some of Greece's best beaches, a fascinatingly intact medieval city, more sunshine than any other Greek island and, in Lindos, the most picturesque of island village resorts as well as the most luxurious and modern five-star hotels in Greece.

The eponymous capital of the island is really two towns rolled into one. The restored medieval quarter, within the 14th-century ring of walls built by the Knights of St John, is an eye-catching mix of historic buildings, museums, colourful shopping streets and unchanged old-fashioned homes and workshops in narrow alleys. Plentiful palm trees plus mosques and minarets (a few still used by the city's handful of Muslims) give the old quarter a distinctly eastern flavour.

In classical times, the island was divided between three powerful city states – Ialissos, Lindos and Kameiros – which banded together in 408 BC to build a new capital, Rhodes, on the site of today's city. Remnants of the ancient capital can be seen on the slopes of Monte Smith and at a newly discovered site on Odos Panetiou.

The new town, built around the Mandraki harbour, is a more commonplace blend of homes, shops, hotels, restaurants, bars and discos

A bronze deer, the emblem of Rhodes, stands guard over Mandraki harbour

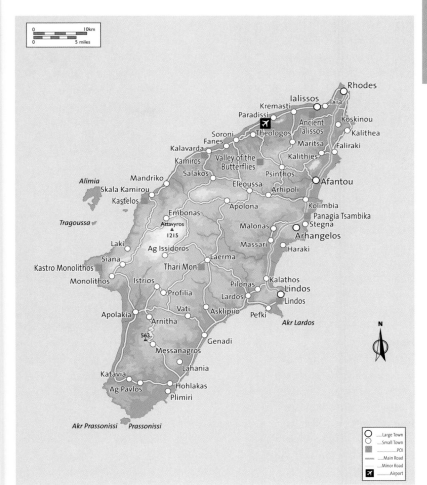

behind a rather grand waterfront of pompous Italianate public buildings and arcaded cafés.

Large holiday resorts spread either side of Rhodes Town on both the east and west coasts, and Lindos is the hub of a second concentration of resort beaches. The west coast, often windswept where it is not mountainous, is less visited, and inland, especially in the south, is a different world of rolling hills and farms.

Rhodes's smaller satellites, the islands of Simi, Halki and Tilos, are within easy reach by hydrofoil, fast catamaran or ferry, and a small fleet of excursion vessels sets out each morning from Mandraki harbour.

Afantou

Popular Afantou, with its long shingle beach, is less crowded than other beaches nearer Rhodes Town and is somewhat less built-up. Small pebbly coves at either end offer potential privacy.

22km (14 miles) south of Rhodes Town.

Faliraki

The island's biggest and noisiest resort appeals to an international clientele in search of watersports, beach life and a vivacious after-dark scene. The beach, long and of coarse sand, with an excellent choice of watersports, is the main attraction and is crowded for almost the whole season.

East coast, 12km (7 miles) south of Rhodes Town.

Haraki

An unexploited fishing hamlet, Haraki has an excellent empty sweep of clean, pebbly beach beside its little harbour. The shell of a small castle of the Knights, on a low hill at its north end, adds a touch of historic colour.

East coast, 40km (25 miles) south of Rhodes Town.

Ialissos

Foundations of a 3rd-century BC Temple of Athene and Zeus, and a particularly fine example of a Doric well-house from 300 BC are highlights of this site.

15km (9 miles) southwest of Rhodes Town. Tel: (22410) 21954. Open: Tue–Sun 8.30am–3pm. Admission charge.

Ixia

The first resort outside Rhodes Town on the west coast is fast turning into a virtual suburb of the city. Most of the island's international luxury-class hotels, with amenities such as landscaped grounds and swimming pools, are located here – just as well, since the beach here, although long, is narrow and gritty.

West coast, 3–4km (2–2^1/$_2$ miles) south of Rhodes Town.

Kamiros

The graceful columns and foundations of the ancient city of Kamiros are located within walls constructed later in medieval times. They have been excavated and partly restored by Italian archaeologists.

35km (22 miles) southwest of Rhodes Town, signposted from main coast road. Tel: (22410) 75674. Open: Tue–Sun 8.30am–3pm. Admission charge.

Lindos

The prettiest village on Rhodes and one of the most charming in Greece, Lindos is noted for its unique homes, built around courtyards with elaborate mosaics in black and white pebbles. Traffic is banned in the village centre, and the little village is completely taken over by tourism.

Acropolis

The Acropolis of Lindos is built on a 180m (591ft)-high sea cliff, protected by impregnable 15th-century

Graceful 3rd-century BC columns mark the site of the Temple of Apollo on Monte Smith

battlements. The Gothic gate and stair and a partially ruined church of St John stand among the ruins of the 5th-century BC temple precinct ruins. High points are the 2nd-century BC 'Ship of Lindos', a relief of a galley carved into the rock by the main gate, and on the highest point the columns of the 4th-century BC Doric Temple of Athene.

Within the walls of the castle, immediately above the village, signposted. Tel: (22410) 75674. Open: Tue–Sun 8.30am–8pm. Admission charge.

Kastro Monolithos (Monolithos Castle)

This ghostly, abandoned 15th-century castle was built by the Knights on a pine-covered crag to watch over the southern part of the west coast.

83km (52 miles) southwest of Rhodes Town, signposted. Free admission.

Petaloudes (Valley of the Butterflies)

Despite the valley's popular name, the colourful scarlet-winged insects which swarm here in July and August are in fact tiger moths. Outside the moth season, when no coach parties visit the valley, it is a pleasant green retreat.

26km (16 miles) southwest of Rhodes Town. Tel: (22410) 81801. Open: 9am–6pm. Admission charge.

Monte Smith

Three slender 3rd-century BC columns on the hillside mark the site of the Temple of Apollo and the ancient acropolis of Rhodes. Below them is the restored 3rd-century BC stadium and *odeion* (theatre).

1km (²/₃ mile) southwest of Rhodes Town. Tel: (22410) 25500. Open: 8.30am–8pm. Free admission.

Walk: Rhodes Old Town

This walk takes in the best features of the picturesque old quarter, with a look at ancient relics, medieval fortifications and Turkish survivals. High points include the various inns (headquarters and lodgings) of the 'tongues' of the Knights and the restored Palace of the Grand Masters.

Allow 2½ hours, plus half an hour for the Archaeological Museum and time for shopping on Odos Sokratous.

1 Pili Navarhiou

Enter the Old Town by Pili Navarhiou (Admiral's Gate), off the south end of Mandraki harbour. An arched stone bridge crosses the dry moat.
Pass through the arched gateway which pierces the massive walls to enter Platia Alexandrou.

2 Inn of Auvergne

The arched doorway of the 14th-century inn leads into a courtyard with a fountain made of marble blocks taken from early Byzantine churches. The Inn of Auvergne is on the east side of the square. On the west is the 14th-century Arsenal (armoury)

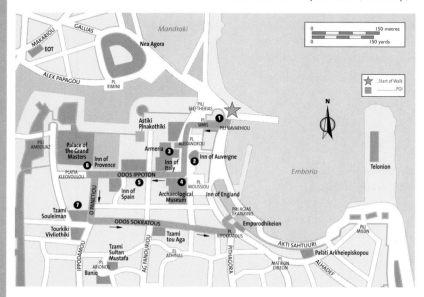

of the Knights, now the Museum of Decorative Arts.

3 Armeria (Arsenal) and Museum of Decorative Arts

The arms of Roger de Pinsot, Grand Master of the Knights of St John from 1355 to 1365, stand above the doorway. The museum contains fine Rhodian pottery, furniture and costumes.

Leaving Platia Alexandrou by the southwest corner, pause at the Archaeological Museum before turning right on to the long cobbled prospect of Odos Ippoton.

4 Archaeological Museum

The Archaeological Museum is housed in the former Hospital of the Knights, a grand Gothic building dating from the late 15th century and displaying the arms of Jean de Lastic, Grand Master from 1437 to 1454. The museum, housed on the lower floor, displays a fine assortment of statuary, including the masterly *Aphrodite of Rhodes*, a 1st-century BC statue of the goddess.

5 Odos Ippoton (Street of the Knights)

The eight different 'tongues' all had their lodges (or inns) on this long street, leading uphill from the Hospital and Arsenal to the Palace of the Grand Masters. Turrets, gargoyles and carved coats of arms above each arched doorway mark the inns of each 'tongue'.

6 Palace of the Grand Masters

Square towers, crenellated walls and sturdy bastions protect the fortress-like palace. The first-floor state rooms contain marvellously restored mosaics. *Walk 250m (275yds) south on Odos Panetiou. The dome of Tzami Souleiman (Mosque of Suleiman) is at the end.*

7 Tzami Souleiman (Mosque of Suleiman)

The building, converted into a mosque in 1522 following Suleiman's conquest of the city, is elegantly decorated in pale yellow and pink. It has a fine Italian Renaissance gate.

Turn left on to Odos Sokratous, the town's main shopping street, lined with jewellers, antique and souvenir shops, designer clothes stalls and leather boutiques. At the foot of Sokratous, leave the old town by Pili Agias Ekaterinis.

Rhodes Old Town is a living museum of medieval buildings

Mosques and Muslims

Minarets and domes among the palm trees are a reminder of Rhodes' Turkish past. Unlike mosques elsewhere in the islands, some of those on Rhodes are still used by worshippers. Rhodes has quite a large Muslim population, originally dating from the 16th-century conquest, and boosted in 1913 by Greek and Turkish Muslims driven from their homes on Crete in an early act of ethnic cleansing following its union with Greece. They settled in Rhodes, and the Nea Kritika (New Cretan) district on the road to the airport is still a largely Muslim community.

The colourful Tzami Souleiman (Mosque of Suleiman) is one of Rhodes Old Town's major landmarks, while the leaning, turban-topped headstones of the overgrown Muslim cemetery (near the junction of Eleftherias and Vassileos Konstantinou, west of Mandraki harbour) are another relic.

The Mosque of Suleiman was built anew to mark the Turkish conquest of the island by Suleiman the Magnificent in 1522, but many other mosques in the Turkish quarter were originally Orthodox churches, and fine Byzantine frescoes have been discovered beneath plaster in the disused Pegial el Din and Ilk Mihrab mosques.

On Sokratous, the shopping street in the heart of the Old Town, the Tzami tou Aga mosque is still used by local devout Muslims, and other surviving mosques, such as Platia Aronos, in the old quarter, are dotted around the Old Town, which became a purely Muslim quarter after the Turkish conquest.

The restored minaret of the Mosque of Suleiman in Rhodes Old Town

Greece's Muslim legacy can be seen on islands such as Kastellorizon, where this old mosque stands beside the harbour

Northeast Aegean islands

The islands of the northeast Aegean are more remote from Athens and further from each other than those of the cluttered southern waters. Each has its own strong identity, and the region offers a rich choice of scenic splendours, from the verdant vineyards of Samos to the rocky magnificence of Mount Fengari on Samothraki and the treeless hills of Limnos.

Striking village architecture, broad landscapes and a wealth of medieval sights add to the highly individual charm of each island, while the long coastlines hide many of Greece's least-explored beaches.

Fertile farmlands make the larger northeastern isles prosperous – Samos is famous for its wine, and Lesvos (Lesbos) and Hios are renowned for their *ouzo*. Life here has been kinder than on less favoured islands.

The Turkish coast is never far off – it lies within a few kilometres of Lesvos, Samos and Hios – and a strong military presence on several of the islands is a constant reminder of the continuing tension. Since oil was discovered beneath the ocean floor (Greece's only oil rig stands off Thassos), Turkey has renewed claims to mineral rights on the continental shelf. These claims are strenuously denied by Greece.

The northeast Aegean islands joined free Greece only in 1912, after the Greek victory in the First Balkan War.

SAMOS

Samos is the most popular holiday island in the northeast Aegean and one of Greece's most startlingly beautiful islands. To anyone arriving from the stark, arid landscapes of the Cyclades or the Dodecanese, Samos is strikingly verdant, with dark green cypress spires rising from slopes covered with poplars, plane trees and creepers.

Set among this natural beauty are prosperous villages which, with their red tiles, white walls and square stone-built bell towers, could be in Italy.

The island's abundant greenery owes much to its geology: streams and springs emerge from its granite rock to water the vineyards that account for much of the island's income, and Samaina, the dry white wine made by the Coopératives des Vinicoles de Samos (Samos Viticulturists' Cooperatives), is perhaps the only Greek wine that will bear international comparison.

In antiquity, and especially under the rule of Polykrates (*c.* 536–522 BC),

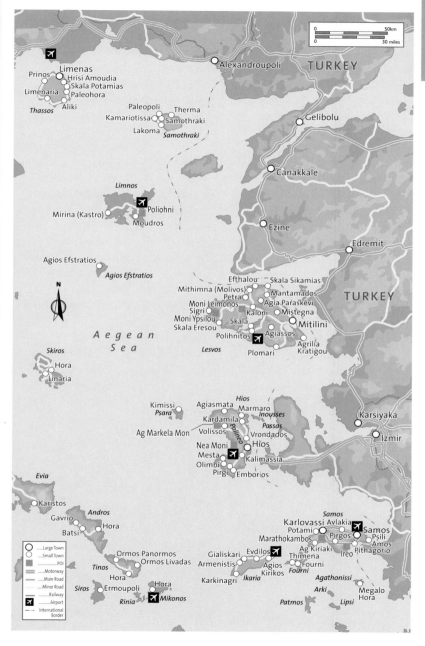

Samos was a great naval power. It entered the 'tourism' business early, for it was already a popular holiday destination in the Roman era of the 2nd and 1st centuries BC. After rule by the Byzantines, Franks, Venetians and Genoese, it fell to the Turks in 1475, and despite gaining limited self-rule after 1832 – as an autonomous principality within the Ottoman empire – it did not officially join Greece until 1913.

Surprisingly, Samos has little to show for its glorious and exciting past. Its charm lies instead in its landscapes and in its beaches, which include lovely stretches of dazzling white pebbles on the north coast and some excellent sandy strands on the eastern and southern shores.
210km (130 miles) east of Pireas.

Samos (Vathi)

The island's capital straddles a long inlet at the eastern end of the north coast. Built in the 19th century, its neoclassical buildings with their grandiose façades, the fountain and palm trees in the waterfront *platea* have a certain faded elegance.

Archaeological Museum

Two buildings, the Old Museum, built in 1912, and the New Museum, which opened in 1987, house a collection which includes the largest known free-standing Greek statue, a 5m (16ft)-tall figure of a youth, apparently dedicated to Apollo, excavated at the Ireo site. The cauldrons, decorated with bronze gryphons, on display here are unique to Samos.
In the square at the east end of Kapetan Katavani. Tel: (22730) 27469.
Open: daily (summer only)
8.30am–3pm. Admission charge.

Byzantine Museum

An assortment of icons, chalices, holy vessels, bones of saints and parchment manuscripts is on display here.

Samos

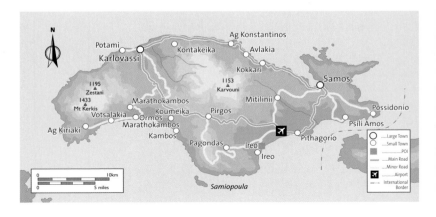

The small castle at Pithagorio overlooks the sea

*In the Mitropoli (Cathedral), one block
back from the waterfront, between
Asklipiadou and 28 Oktobriou.
Tel: (22730) 27312. Open: Tue–Sun
8.30am–3pm. Admission charge.*

Municipal Art Gallery

Collection of portraits of grandly
dressed princes of 19th-century Samos
and bewhiskered heroes of the War of
Independence (1821–30).
*Above the post office in the square at the
eastern end of Kapetan Katavani, next to
the town hall. Open: daily 8.30am–3pm.
Free admission.*

Kokkari

A delightfully picturesque fishing
village-cum-resort, recognisable from
scores of postcards and holiday
brochures. There are pebbly beaches
and coves to the west of the village.
*20km (12 miles) west of Samos, on the
north coast.*

Agios Konstantinos

A leafy Italianate village spread out along several kilometres of pebble beach on the main north coast road, Agios Konstantinos is near Kokkari, the start for exploring the cypress-covered slopes and network of paths inland (*see pp130–31*). *Midway along the north coast.*

Karlovassi

The island's sprawling western port and commercial centre has few sights of note, though two snarling Venetian marble lions stand in its public gardens, near the town centre. Karlovassi's main importance is that it is an arrival and departure point for island-hopping. *45km (28 miles) west of Samos, on the north coast.*

Mount Kerkis

The bald grey summit of Kerkis, often swathed in white cloud, dominates all of western Samos and can be seen clearly from neighbouring Ikaria and Fourni. Keen walkers with adequate footwear, good maps and mountain experience can tackle the 1,433m (4,701ft) ascent from the south coast road, not far from Votsalakia.

Ormos Marathokambos

This pleasant, peaceful village still has a thriving boatbuilding industry which turns out traditional wooden caiques for local fishermen, but in recent years it has also become the gateway to a string of small resorts scattered along the excellent sand-and-pebble beaches

that stretch off to the west. The closest of these is Votsalakia, about 1.6km (1 mile) to the west, while Psili Amos and Limnionas lie a little further on. Along each beach is a scattering of small hotels, small-scale self-catering apartment blocks, shops and tavernas. Confusingly, Samos has two beaches called Psili Amos (which means 'silver bay') – one here, the other at the other end of the south coast, 8km (5 miles) east of Pithagorio. Head east from Ormos to discover a long and usually completely empty pebble beach, behind which is a delta of lush farmland. *20km (12 miles) south of Karlovassi.*

Ireo

A thriving resort with small hotels and tavernas has sprung up along the pebbly beach beside the ancient Temple of Hera (wife of Zeus) which stands beside the sea here.

Ireo is Samos's most important classical site, and is extremely old, with traces of Mycenaean settlement as early as the second millennium BC. For casual visitors, though, the single remaining column of the great 23m (75ft)-high temple which once stood here is the main landmark. Various graffitists through the ages have carved their names or initials into the white marble, but there's not much else to see and you can enjoy the sight of the column from outside the enclosure without paying to enter. *500m (550yds) east of the modern village*

The port of Pithagorio

of Ireo. Open: Apr–Oct Tue–Sun 8am–7.30pm. Admission charge. Sometimes closed for new excavation.

Pithagorio

The third of Samos's three ports is only 10km (6 miles) from the Turkish coast and is the departure point for day trips to the ancient Greek cities of Ionia on the modern Turkish coast. Tavernas cluster the quayside of an enormous harbour where yachts outnumber fishing boats. The remnants of the 6th-century BC city walls can be seen curving around the harbour and the hills behind the village. These are almost the only indication that this is the site of the great ancient city of Samos. Pithagorio has been so-named since 1955, after Pythagoras, the classical-era mathematician and philosopher who formulated the famous theorem that the square on the hypotenuse of a right-angled triangle is equal to the sum of the squares on the other two sides. Born here in the 6th century BC and a protégé of the tyrant Polykrates, he later emigrated to the Greek colonies in southern Italy. *Southeast corner of Samos.*

Archaeological Museum

Finds from the Ireo site (*see p118*), including busts of Roman emperors and a 1st-century BC statue of Augustus Caesar, are the highlights.
In village hall. Tel: (22730) 61400.
Open: Tue–Sun 8.30am–3pm.
Free admission.

Castle of Likourgos Logothetis

This miniature castle was built in 1824 by the leader of the island's rebellion against the Turks. Around it are the remains of colonnaded houses from the Roman era.
In the centre of the village, 400m (440yds) west of the harbour. Open: only for performances.

Samiopoula

The uninhabited islet of Samiopoula nestles close to its parent island, Samos. Covered in pines, and with several pretty pebbly coves, it is a pleasant destination for picnics, swimming and snorkelling trips, which are usually organised by boat operators from Pithagorio to its east and Ormos Marathokambos to its west.
5km (3 miles) south of Ormos Marathokambos.

IKARIA

Long, thin and very mountainous, Ikaria lies midway between green Samos and chic Mikonos (*see pp59–61*), and most island-hoppers bypass it on their way from one to the other. It is said to be where Ikaros (Icarus), son of the legendary Minoan inventor Dedalos (Daedalus), plummeted to his death after flying too close to the sun, thereby melting the wax which held his newly made wings together. Others who have landed here unwillingly include the composer of the ubiquitous theme tune from *Zorba the Greek*, Mikis Theodorakis, one of many left-wing dissidents confined to Ikaria by pre- and post-war dictatorships.

Ikaria's south coast looks like one long cliff, with its only anchorage at Agios Kirikos, the island's main port and capital, at its east end. The north coast is almost equally rugged, but the cliffs are broken by deltas of farmland at the mouths of steep valleys. The extensive pine woodlands of Ikaria's inland plateau have been badly damaged by fire, but the island's hinterland is otherwise surprisingly verdant. Like Samos, it is watered by small, constantly flowing streams.
30km (19 miles) west of Samos; 50km (31 miles) east of Mikonos.

Agios Kirikos

Ikaria's capital, a sleepy village of tumbledown houses, overlooks a fishing harbour and a little-used ferry port.
East end of the south coast.

Armenistis

A fishing hamlet and a row of tavernas overlook a north-facing bay and the best beaches on the island: two long stretches of coarse white sand.
44km (27 miles) west of Agios Kirikos.

Evdilos

This once-derelict ferry port on the north coast of the island has come back to life thanks to tourism.
33km (21 miles) northwest of Agios Kirikos.

Nas

Nas is little more than a name on the map: three tavernas cater for campers and sunbathers on the (unofficial) nudist beach in a pebbly, cliff-ringed cove.
4km (2¹/₂ miles) west of Armenistis.

Naos Artemis Tavropoliou (Sanctuary of Artemis of the Bulls)

Impressive, stepped foundations of this temple overlook a reed-fringed pool.
Immediately above the beach at Nas. Free admission.

HIOS (Chios)

Hios is a long, crescent-shaped island close to the Turkish coast. Its biggest attractions lie in the high, rolling hinterland of the south, where a handful of unique fortified villages are hidden in fertile pockets among steep hillsides. The island has no outstanding ancient sites, but it possesses a wealth of medieval sites from a richly textured past which blends Byzantine, Venetian Genoese and Turkish influences.

A century of Venetian rule (1204–1304) was followed by the long reign of the Genoese Giustiniani family (1346–1566). From the early 15th century, however, Hios came under Ottoman rule. The massacre of over 25,000 islanders after a failed revolt in 1822 was immortalised by the French painter Eugène Delacroix (1798–1863) and hardened European support for Greece against the Turks.

The majority of the island's most interesting sights and its best beaches are in the southern half of the island, south and west of the capital, Hios.
75km (47 miles) south of Lesvos.

Hios (Hora)

The capital is a busy commercial port and is not much concerned with tourism, though a handful of old streets and buildings lend it character.
Midway along the east coast, facing Turkey.

The 11th-century New Monastery on Hios stands among cypress trees

Dimotikos Kipos (Public Gardens)

A ring of mature palms surrounds a pair of marble heraldic gryphons and a heroic bronze statue of Konstantinos Kanaris (1822), one of the leaders in the War of Independence.

Town centre. Free admission.

Kastro (Castle)

The dilapidated walls of the castle quarter (now being restored in places) enclose tumbledown Turkish shophouses of great charm. The turban-topped tombstones of a Turkish cemetery, shaded by palms, mark the corner of Odos Mit Arseniou and Odos Tzon Kenenty (John Kennedy), while the clustered domes of a derelict medieval *hammam* (Turkish bath) may be seen built into the ramparts at the north end of Navarchos Nikodimou. Ringed by a now-dry moat, the castle was built in the 10th century AD by the Byzantines and added to by later conquerors.

West end of Neoreion, one block west of the waterfront. Open: daily 8.30am–3pm. Free admission.

Medjitie Djami
(Post-Byzantine Museum)

The courtyard of this former mosque encloses a fascinating array of objects, from green bronze cannon bearing Venetian crests, to Jewish and Turkish tombstones.

Kanari 9, opposite public gardens. Tel: (22710) 26866. Open: daily 8.30am–3pm.

Moussio Philippos Argentis
(Philip Argentis Museum)

A rich collection of etchings, drawings, traditional costumes and wooden furniture and utensils.

Korai 2, in the Bibliothiki Khiou Korai (Korai Library). Tel: (22710) 28256. Open: Mon–Fri 8am–2pm & 5–8.30pm, Sat 8am–12.30pm. Admission charge.

Mastikohoria

The so-called 'mastic villages' of southern Hios are unique, labyrinthine communities, fortified for easy defence against raiders. Many of the villagers still make their living from harvesting the chewy gum of the mastic bush, which grows semi-wild all over this part of the island. In medieval times it was highly valued and it is still used today as a base for sweets, perfumes, and a liqueur which is unique to Hios and is claimed to have medicinal properties.

Mesta

Mesta is the best preserved of the mastic villages, with a maze of warmly coloured stone alleyways and arches surrounding a lovely central square surrounded by old-fashioned cafés.

10km (6 miles) northwest of Pirgi.

Olimbi

Olimbi has grown up around a 13th-century core of walls, with a 20m (66ft) defensive tower in its central square. An arched gateway, Kato Porta (Lower Gate), was originally the only way into

the village, and could be barred against attackers.
5km (3 miles) northwest of Pirgi.

Pirgi

Pirgi is the most striking of the mastic villages. Many of the tall, balconied houses in its maze of streets and alleys are covered with elaborate, geometrical designs in black and white (called *xista*), while clusters of tomatoes and peppers, hung up to dry from balconies, add splashes of vermilion.
35km (22 miles) southwest of Hios town.

LESVOS (Lesbos)

Lesvos, the third largest of all the Greek islands and one of the most populous – with 105,000 people in its 1,630sq km (629sq miles) – has a bit of everything. There are fine beaches on its 370km (230-mile)-long coastline, some of them busy, others quite deserted. There are rolling hills covered with olive groves and pastoral lowlands, arid semi-desert landscapes interspersed by oasis-like valleys and bald summits emerging from pine-forested foothills. There are quiet fishing harbours, even quieter farming villages in the hills, and one breathtakingly pretty historic town turned resort. It even has its own 'sea', the mirror-calm Kolpos Kallonis, which plunges deeply into the southern coastline. There are some 11 million olive trees, and road verges are often lined with yellow clusters of aniseed, a reminder that Lesvos produces some of Greece's best *ouzo*.

Mithimna on Lesvos

75km (47 miles) southeast of Limnos; 240km (149 miles) northeast of Athens.

Mithimna (Molivos)

A delightful, charmingly preserved village of pink and grey stone mansions with bright red, green, yellow and blue woodwork climbs up to the battlements and circular bastions of the Genoese castle – a dramatic sight when floodlit at night. A pebble-and-sand beach runs along the bay east of the village, and fishing boats bob in the small harbour.
62km (39 miles) northwest of Mitilini.

Frourio Molivou (Molivos Fortress)

From the battlements, there are fine views of the village, the surrounding hills and the nearby Turkish coast.
Above the village. Open: Tue–Sun 7.30am–8pm. Free admission.

Moni Leimonos (Limonos Monastery)

Constructed in 1527, this is a graceful, rambling building of decorative brick cloisters and grey and pink stone. Its museum displays embroidered robes and crowns, icons and reliquaries.
45km (28 miles) west of Mitilini, 400m (440yd) south of main east–west road. Open: 9am–1pm & 5–7.30pm. Admission charge to museum.

Moni Ypsilou (Ipsilo Monastery)

A fortified eyrie, dedicated to Ayios Ioannis Theologos (St John the Divine). Arcaded cells surround a cobbled courtyard and church, and its walls are partly decorated with bright blue tiles.

Tall, 19th-century buildings overlook Mitilini's long sweep of waterfront

A small museum on the second floor displays gorgeous embroidered vestments and illustrated manuscripts.
80km (50 miles) west of Mitilini on the road to Sigri. Open: daily. Free admission to the museum.

Mitilini

The island capital is a commercial centre with a population of 25,000. Its visitor appeal is threefold – a bustling, eastern-flavoured bazaar area along Odos Ermou, an impressive stronghold and several excellent museums.

Archaeological Museum

Statues, pottery and other finds from local sites.
South end of 8 Novembriou. Tel: (22510) 28032. Open: Tue–Sun 8.30am–3pm. Admission charge.

Kastro (Castle)

Reconstructed by the Genoese Gattelusi family in 1373, crumbling walls surround the hilltop crowned by massive round towers.
On the eastern promontory, north of the ferry harbour. Open: daily 8am–2.30pm. Admission charge.

Moussio Laikis Technis (Museum of Folk Art)

Village costumes and other memorabilia in a charmingly restored former harbourmaster's office (Old Museum). Part of the collection has been moved to a new building nearby (New Museum).

Platia Sapphous, on the waterfront.
Tel: (22510) 41388. Open: daily
8.30am–3pm. Admission charge.

Theophilos Museum
The self-taught Naïve painter
Theophilos (1873–1934), who was born
on Lesvos, wandered all over Greece
painting. This collection includes more
than 80 of his landscapes, scenes from
mythology, folklore and village life.
4km (2¹/₂ miles) from the town centre in
Varia suburb, signposted. Tel: (22510)
41644. Open: Tue–Sun 9am–1pm &
4.30–8pm. Admission charge.

Petra
A long, coarse-sand beach and small
resort popular for its proximity to
Mithimna.
5km (3 miles) south of Mithimna.

Skala Eresou (Eressos)
A small resort on the island's best
beach, backed by harsh mountains and
an oasis-like delta of fertile farmland.
92km (57 miles) southwest of Mitilini.

LIMNOS (Lemnos)
The rolling hills of Limnos are covered
with a golden fuzz of pasture and grain
fields. It is one of the richest agricultural
islands, dotted with derelict windmills.
   Ormos Moudrou (Moudros Bay)
takes a huge bite out of the south coast.
This vast, well-sheltered natural
harbour made Limnos a strategic base
for the British fleet during the Gallipoli
campaign of 1915, for the Turkish coast

and the Dardanelles are only 60km (37
miles) to the east. For the same reason,
Limnos remains highly militarised, with
Greek army and navy installations on
most of its hilltops and anchorages.
75km (47 miles) northwest of Lesvos;
270km (168 miles) northeast of Pireas.

Mirina
The island's cheerfully old-fashioned
but well-kept main town is guarded by
a Venetian castle, and has two accessible
beaches. The bazaar-like shopping area
is lined with charming old-fashioned
shop-houses.

Archaeological Museum
Stone Age and Bronze Age finds from
sites around the island.
On the Romaikos beachfront, 1km
(²/₃ mile) west of the harbour.
Tel: (22540) 22900. Open: Tue–Sun
8.30am–3pm. Admission charge.

Frourio Nepheli (Nepheli Fortress)
A 13th-century Venetian castle with
towers and battlements still intact,
dramatically located on a crag.
500m (550yds) west of harbour.
Open: sunrise–sunset. Free admission.

Poliohni
Traces of one of the oldest settlements
in Greece, dating from the fourth
millennium BC, are clearly visible here.
33km (21 miles) east of Mirina, 3km
(2 miles) east of Kaminia village,
signposted. Tel: (22540) 91249. Open:
Tue–Sun 8.30am–3pm. Free admission.

SAMOTHRAKI

The egg-shaped isle of Samothraki rises to the central peak of Mount Fengari, the highest mountain in the Aegean islands at 1,611m (5,285ft). On its lower northern slopes lies fertile farmland where almost all the island's people work and live. The grain fields, sheepfolds and dense woodland of this well-watered north coast are in sharp contrast to the jagged outlines of Fengari's peaks and the near-desert wilderness of the southeast of the island.

45km (28 miles) south of the mainland port of Alexandroupoli.

Kamariotissa

The island's main village is close to its western tip. Ferries and hydrofoils link Samothraki to the mainland and to the isles to the north and south.

Close to the western tip of the island.

Paleopoli

This is the site of the island's original capital, abandoned in the post-Byzantine period, and now the location of the most impressive archaeological site in the northeast Aegean.

Arkheologiko Moussio (Archaeological Museum)

Finds from the site include altars and friezes, votive offerings, lovely delicate Roman glassware, tinsel-like gold jewellery, 5th-century BC black-figure pottery columns from the Rotunda of

THE CULT OF THE GREAT GODS

The colonists from Samos who arrived on Samothraki around 700 BC found that the island was already settled by earlier people who had their own religion.

The Samians absorbed the local gods into their own pantheon, creating in the process the hybrid cult of the Great Gods, and they built a vast sanctuary to serve as their place of worship.

The cult survived for almost a millennium, remaining popular well into Roman times, partly because, unlike other cults of the time, it was open to women and slaves, as well as the ruling class.

Its pantheon was descended from pre-Greek Thracian fertility deities and included the Great Mother, a consort named Kadmilos and two enigmatic intercessor gods, the Kabiroi. These gods were later identified with the Dioscuri of the classical Greek pantheon.

Arsinoë and a replica of the Winged Victory of Samothraki (the original was removed by French archaeologists in 1863 and is now in the Louvre, Paris).

6km (4 miles) northeast of Kamariotissa, signposted from the coast road.
Tel: (25510) 41474. Open: daily 8.30am–3pm.

Ieron ton Megalon Theon (Sanctuary of the Great Gods)

The huge hillside site is second only to the Minoan sites on Crete for sheer impact. High points include the plinth of the Rotunda of Arsinoë and the five surviving columns of the Hieron, plus remnants of the theatre, the sanctuary's massive fortifications and other shrines.

6km (4 miles) northeast of Kamariotissa, signposted to the Archaeological Museum from the coast road. Open: daily 8.30am–3pm. Admission charge.

Samothraki Town (Hora)

Samothraki's tiny medieval capital stands at the head of a hidden valley on the lower slopes of the island's central massif. It is a pretty jumble of two-storey white stone houses with painted shutters and red-tiled roofs, crowned by a ruined Byzantine-Genoese castle.
5km (3 miles) from Kamariotissa.

Kastro (Castle)

Round and square bastions surround a tiny square inner keep with a beautiful view down into a wooded valley to the sea and over to the coast of Thrace (Thraki) on the mainland. Marble slabs carved with Byzantine inscriptions and heraldic devices decorate the walls. The lower storey is the police station.
On the crag above the village. Free admission.

Laografiko Moussio (Folk Museum)

Traditional implements include a wooden loom and spinning wheel, plus pottery and vividly coloured embroidery.
Above the public library, by the main square and immediately below the Church of the Virgin. Tel: (25510) 41227.

Marble columns stand above the Sanctuary of the Great Gods

Open: daily 9am–2pm & 5–9pm. Admission charge.

Naos tis Koimisis tis Theotokou (Church of the Assumption of the Virgin)

This enormous, whitewashed church, built in 1875, houses the skulls of the Five Martyrs of Samothraki, early Christian saints of the Orthodox faith. *Centre of the village. If closed, enquire at the public library next door for keys.*

THASSOS

A circular island of low hills and gentle valleys, Thassos is one of Greece's greener isles – though not as green as it once was. Its pine forests are only now recovering from forest fires which struck in the 1980s, and many of its slopes are cloaked in young, newly planted trees. A single road makes a 100km (62-mile) circuit round Thassos, with giddying switchbacks through the hills of the east coast.

Thassos has a couple of quiet resorts and one outstanding beach, but hasn't yet been discovered by tourism in a big way, despite the fact that international charter flights bring package tourists to mainland Kavala, a mere 30-minute ferry hop away. *25km (16 miles) southeast of mainland port of Kavala.*

Limenas (Thassos Town)

Thassos Town, the island's capital, is located on a double bay facing the mainland (at its nearest it is only 11km/ 7 miles away), with a deep modern ferry harbour and a shallow old harbour.

It is a pleasant, sleepy little modern town that is ringed by ancient walls, dotted with spectacular Hellenic remains and overlooked by a medieval castle. The massive walls of ancient Thassos date from 495 BC and form a 2km (1¼-mile) hilltop ring around Limin (don't confuse Limenas with Limenaria). *North coast of Thassos.*

Agioi Apostoloi (Holy Apostles)

A small, modern, whitewashed church stands amid the ruins and columns of an early Christian basilica, itself built from remnants of a pre-Christian shrine. *On the headland above the boatyard, 500m (550yds) east of the old harbour. Free admission.*

Agora (Ancient Marketplace)

The grand ground plan of Hellenic (3rd to 1st century BC) Thassos can clearly be seen, with column bases marking the arcades of the great *stoas* and other buildings. *By the old harbour. Open: Mon–Fri 8.30am–5pm. Admission charge.*

Ancient Theatre

This marble-tiered theatre is still used in summer, when music and drama performances take advantage of the perfect acoustics. *750m (820yds) above the agora. Free admission.*

and small hotels, along a sandy bay on the south coast.
55km (34 miles) south of Thassos Town.

Thassos is picturesque and little visited

Archaeological Museum

This fine collection includes the *Kriophoros of Thassos*, a giant archaic statue, dating from the 6th century BC, of a naked youth carrying a ram to sacrifice. There are also terracotta works and marble and ivory carvings.
Next to the agora. Tel: (25930) 22180. Open: Tue–Sun 8.30am–3pm. Admission charge.

Kastro (Castle)

The battlements of a medieval Genoese castle surmount the city walls at their highest point.
1km (²/₃ mile) west of Agioi Apostoloi, 250m (275yds) from Archaio Theatro. Free admission.

Limenaria

The island's biggest holiday resort comprises a cluster of shops, tavernas

Aliki

This delightful one-time fishing hamlet is no more than a row of white cottages roofed with slabs of grey stone. It is situated on a tiny isthmus leading to a pine-covered headland, hemmed in by a diminutive sandy beach on its west side, with a clear bay and a pebbly beach on its east flank.
52km (32 miles) south of Thassos Town by road.

Sanctuary of the Dioscuri

Column stumps, walls and foundations and a stone sarcophagus mark this 7th-century BC site. On the headland immediately above are the ruins of two 5th-century AD Christian churches.
50m (55yds) west of the village, signposted. Free admission.

Hrisi Amoudia

This gorgeous sweep of coarse white sand and clear water is ringed by dramatic, pine-clad limestone cliffs rising towards the 1,204m (3,950ft) peak of Ypsario and the 1,100m (3,609ft) summit of Profitis Ilias. The small resort of Hrisi Amoudia is at the north end of the beach, with a gaggle of tavernas and houses. Another resort, Skala Potamias, lies at the south end.
7–9km (4–5¹/₂ miles) from Thassos Town.

Walk: Hills of Samos

The hills rising from the north coast of the island combine verdant woodlands with dramatic mountain views and quaint villages. This walk starts and finishes on the coast. If you start by 9am you should arrive back in Kokkari in time for lunch and a lazy afternoon on the beach. The route may be slightly altered by newly built dirt roads; the walking path is marked with red dots painted on walls and boulders, but you must keep a sharp eye open for these as they can easily be overlooked.

Start at the southwest end of Kokkari, at the junction of the old road through the village and the new bypass, next to the Mios Beach Hotel. Follow the tarred side road which quickly turns into a dirt track, and keep left of the farm fields inland of Kokkari until after 10 minutes the track – now a footpath – passes under a derelict Turkish aqueduct. Continue to follow this trail, crossing two new forestry jeep tracks.

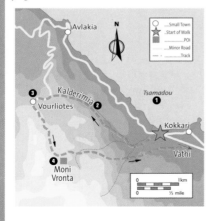

1 Tsamadou

The trail follows the 200m (220yd) contour, with the vivid turquoise bay of Tsamadou and its white pebble beach immediately below, to your right.
Continue across a rocky ravine to the base of the final pitch to Vourliotes village.

2 Kalderimia

The steepest stage of the walk follows one of Samos's surviving *kalderimia*, the painstakingly cobbled mule-paths which once criss-crossed every island but have since been destroyed in many places by new road-building or have simply been neglected.
After 90 minutes, the trail meets the tarred road to Vourliotes. Continue for a further 15 minutes to the village.

3 Vourliotes

The outskirts of Vourliotes are reminiscent of a ghost town, with the tumbledown walls of abandoned houses lining narrow lanes. In the last century, the village had 1,200 inhabitants. It now has fewer than half that number, but streams and fertile land make the remaining inhabitants prosperous by hill-village standards. Stop for a drink and snack in the quaint central square. *Return to Kokkari via the Moni Vronta trail, rising to 500m (1,640ft) above sea level. Head south on the track (signposted and marked with red dots) which leads from the eastern corner of Vourliotes.*

4 Moni Vronta (Our Lady of the Thunder)

The substantial, stone-roofed monastery of Vronta dates from the 16th century, when Samos – which had been deserted for a century because of pirate raids – was resettled by Greeks from Asia Minor under a benevolent

pasha. According to island belief, thunderstorms always follow the festival of the Birth of the Virgin, which is celebrated here and in Vourliotes on 7–8 September each year. (Note: the Greek army sometimes billets troops in the monastery and photography may be banned if they are in residence.) *From Vronta, follow the path downhill and east from the monastery, signposted Monopati Kokkari. The trail follows the right bank of a deep gorge, with sheer cliffs on the opposite side and views down to Kokkari. On a clear day, you can see right across to Turkey.*

After another 45 minutes, the trail cuts across a web of fields and dirt tracks, passes through olive groves, and emerges at a taverna on the main road, 500m (550yds) from Kokkari village centre.

Kokkari, where the walk ends, is a quaint combination of resort and fishing village

Fishermen and boatbuilders

Nylon nets make life easier

Old, gnarled, cross-legged fishermen mending bright yellow or dark crimson nets are one of the everyday sights of the Greek islands, and no island harbour is complete without its flotilla of tiny, brightly painted fishing boats.

Almost all of them bear the names of a local saint, who protects both boat and boatmen. This is a very traditional form of life insurance and is reflected onshore in the tiny chapels dedicated to the Panagia (Virgin), built by grateful fishermen in thanks for their safekeeping and livelihood at sea.

You can see traditional wooden caiques being built and repaired in the harbours of Kokkari and Karlovassi on Samos (see pp117–18), Simi (p155), Limenas (Thassos Town) on Thassos (pp128–9) and at other island ports.

If you look closely at the prow of one of these little vessels, you will often see a diamond shape cut into the wood – a stylised version of the eye painted on the prow of the ancient triremes and a reminder that the captains of these little fishing-boats are descendants of the sailors who trounced the Persian fleet at Salamis.

Much fishing is done at night. Flotillas of dinghies, each carrying a pair of powerful gas lamps, are used to attract squid and small fry into circles of nets. The sound of their engines 'putt-putting' back into harbour at first light starts many an island day.

Another oft-heard harbour sound is the slap of an octopus being tenderised by pounding its rubbery tentacles against a boulder. Octopus are taken with a trident or a formidable triple hook on a handline.

On most islands, the catch is as small as the boats. Overfishing has taken its toll of Aegean stocks. Island boatmen pursue their quarry with everything from fine-mesh nets to spearguns and fish-traps. Dynamite was sometimes used to maximise impact and it is not uncommon to meet an older fisherman who has lost a hand through mishandling of explosives. These days, more environmentally friendly fish farms are widely established in an effort to increase island fish stocks.

Tourism and relative prosperity in Greece itself have played a part in encouraging intensive fishing. Greeks and tourists love fresh fish, and prices for the prized *barbounia* (red mullet) have soared.

Finally, on island beaches you may see fishermen of another sort: young Romeos who spend their summers in pursuit of female tourists are called *kamakia* – 'harpoons'.

A work in progress

Sporades and Evia

There is more variety to be found in the Sporades (Vories Sporades) and Evia than in any other Greek island group. Splashed across some 4,800sq km of the northwest Aegean, but within sight of each other, they include Greece's second-largest island, a scattering of tiny islets which are home to rare birds and sea mammals, and four mid-sized isles, each with a charm all of its own.

Long, sandy beaches lined with bars and sunloungers, empty pebbly strands that are hard to get to, sea-caves and wooded hillsides, lively resorts and tranquil villages can all be found here, and it's easy to combine a holiday on one of these isles with a trip to the nearby mainland or even Athens.

Pine-wooded Skiathos with its fringe of sandy beaches is the best known of the Sporades, partly because it has the only international airport in the group. But its near neighbours, Skopelos and Alonissos, have their charms too, although neither can rival Skiathos's golden strands. Fast catamarans and hydrofoils connect all three with each other and (via Skiathos) the mainland port of Volos, so it's easy to combine two, or even all three, islands into one holiday. Lonely Skiros, some 60km (38 miles) off to the southeast, is larger, more idiosyncratic and less visited than its sisters, and attracts a less rampantly hedonistic clientele. To many people, Evia, the largest island in the group, hardly qualifies as an island at all. The Gulf of Evia, which separates it from the mainland, is only 100m (328ft) wide at its narrowest point and is crossed via a road bridge.

These are not islands that are over-endowed with ancient must-see relics, though all have their share of more recent relics – recent, that is, by Greek standards, as they span all the long centuries of the Byzantine empire, the Venetian occupation and Turkish rule. The real appeal of all of them, however, lies in idyllic beaches, forested hills and rolling landscapes that beckon to walkers, and pristine seas.

SKIATHOS

The finest beaches of powdery yellow sand to be found anywhere in the Greek islands, a pretty, Italianate island capital, lively nightlife and a better-than-average range of accommodation are the keys to Skiathos's popularity – not only with package holidaymakers from northern Europe, but also with summer visitors from mainland Greece, who fill the harbourside café-bars of Skiathos Town in July and August, while the gleaming white motor-yachts of well-off Athenians and Italians line the quayside.

Inland, Skiathos is an island of rolling hills, mostly covered with pine forest. Despite the island's popularity, the resorts scattered along its south coast are pleasantly small-scale and low-key, while the north coast, with its pebble coves and wave-sculpted rock formations, is still almost undeveloped.

Almost all of the island's 4,000 inhabitants live in Hora (Skiathos Town), which is replete with restaurants, bars, shops and clubs, but most visitors prefer to stay in the resorts. An excellent bus service connects all the resort areas with Hora from early morning until late at night.

Skiathos missed out on the golden age of classical Greece, when it was of little importance. In the 13th century it passed from the Byzantine empire to the Venetians, it was conquered by the Turks in 1538, and finally became part

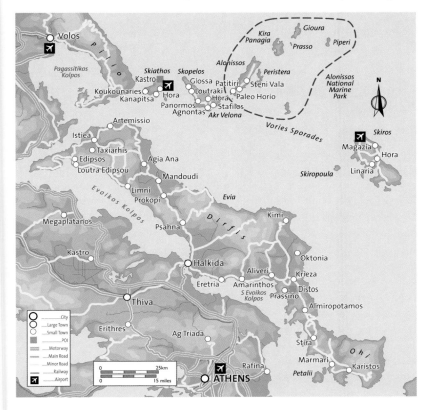

The fertile farmlands of Evia are a chequerboard of grain fields and olive groves

of newly independent Greece in 1828. For sightseers, there are boat trips around the island and to Skopelos, Alonissos and the Alonissos Marine Park; there are also yachts for hire, day trips to the beautiful Pilion peninsula on the mainland, and longer mainland excursions to Athens, the Meteora monasteries and Mt Olympus.

Hora (Skiathos Town)

This is one of the prettiest villages in the Greek isles, and its red-tiled roofs, Italianate church bell towers, houses with wooden shuttered windows, and wrought-iron balconies overflowing with geraniums and bougainvillea give it a special charm. Built in the 1830s – after the islanders moved from their former homes in the fortified hill village of Kastro – the village stands on two low hills, overlooking twin harbours. The Old Port is still home to a flotilla of fishing boats as well as the base for island-circumnavigating boat trips, while the New Port is jam-packed with sailing yachts and huge private cruisers, as well as being where the inter-island ferries dock. Skiathos's airport is a five-minute taxi-ride away, and an esplanade lined with rather classy open-air summer nightspots is just north of the new marina.

An excellent bus service, leaving every 15 minutes throughout the day during summer, connects Hora with all the beach resorts (stops are numbered 1–26 and are no more than 1km/²/₃ mile apart).

Bourtzi

Between Hora's two harbours, the rocky Bourtzi islet is connected to the mainland by a narrow isthmus and covered in pine trees. A small Venetian castle once stood here, guarding the harbour. Little remains except for its foundations, on top of which stand the island's theatre, an open-air café (with great views to the tiny uninhabited islands not far offshore), and a bathing ladder giving access to the clear blue water below.

South end of Ethnarhiou Makariou.

Kastro

A population of several thousand islanders lived behind the walls of this fortified hilltop settlement from the 14th century until the 1830s, when they moved to the more conveniently located new capital at Hora. Now deserted and mostly ruined – except for the sturdy 17th-century church of Pantokrator, also called Christos sto Kastro (Christ's Church in the Castle) – the village is a popular destination for organised tours from Hora and other resorts. It can also easily be visited independently, but you really need a 4WD vehicle to traverse the rough mountain roads.

8km (5 miles) northwest of Hora.

Lalaria

Halfway along the island's north coast, this pebbly beach with its sea-sculpted rocks is hemmed in by white cliffs. Undeveloped as yet, Lalaria receives a daily seaborne invasion of day-trippers from Koukounaries and Hora.

8km (5 miles) north of Hora. Access by boat or unsurfaced road.

Megali Ammos

This long curve of beach starts just five minutes' walk from the village centre and is lined with café-bars, restaurants and watersports outfits. It's even more popular with local families than with visitors, but for those staying in Hora it compares well with other island strands.

400m (440yds) west of the Old Harbour.

Moni Panagia Evangelistria

This 18th-century monastery dedicated to the Virgin, high on the slopes of Mt Mitikas, is well known for its colourful frescoes. Painted in 1822, they are much more intact than those of many older churches. A visit to the monastery is included on most organised trips to Kastro, but you can also get there easily by public bus from Hora.

4km (2¹/₂ miles) north of Hora.

Papadiamantis House Museum

In the northwest corner off a small square just off Hora's main shopping street, this pretty little museum is well worth a look even if you are not fascinated by 19th-century Greek literature. It celebrates the life of Skiathos's most famous son, the author Alexandros Papadiamantis (1851–1911), who lived here until his death, and is a typical island home of the 19th century, with polished wooden floors and ceilings, tiny bedrooms and portraits of the author and his family.

Plateia Papadiamantis. Tel: (24270) 23843. Open: daily 8.30am–1.30pm & 5–8.30pm.

Trion Ierarchon

The grand *campanile* of this church stands on a square immediately above the old harbour and is Hora's most unmistakable landmark. Built in 1846, the church houses an icon of the Virgin which is credited with miraculous powers.

Plateia Trion Ierarchon. Open: daily.

Koukounaries

This huge, south-facing sweep of fine yellow sand may well be the best beach in Greece. Lapped by clear, warm water and backed by pine woods, it forms the core of a resort that stretches for some distance on either side of the beach and reaches out to several smaller, less-crowded spots.

Bus stops 24–26, 32km (20 miles) west of Hora.

Ambelakia

Follow the signposts along the unsurfaced road that leads over the headland to a small crescent of white sand beneath pine-covered slopes, with a small cantina that serves food and rents loungers.

500m (550yds) west of bus stop 26 and the car park, west end of Koukounaries.

Koukounaries beach

More than 1km (²/₃ mile) of gorgeous sand and sea, easily accessed by a beach-long boardwalk that boasts beach bars and snack restaurants,

Koukounaries beach on Skiathos

watersports kiosks, and rank upon rank of sunloungers and umbrellas. Gorgeous though it is, Koukounaries is never less than busy.

Ormos Krassa ('Small Banana')

Skiathos's remotest beaches are 10–15 minutes' walk through the olive groves from family-friendly Koukounaries. 'Big Banana', once a naturist's favourite resort, is now topless but not bottomless; but 'Small Banana', a few hundred metres further on and discreetly tucked away over a rocky headland, is the last refuge on Skiathos of those who seek an all-over tan. 'Big Banana' has a couple of lively cocktail bars and restaurants, as well as a good choice of watersports, while 'Small Banana' has a basic café which rents loungers.
1km (²/₃ mile) west of bus stop 26.

Troulos

This lively little resort stands between two rocky headlands, and is just a stone's throw from Koukounaries and its facilities. There are plenty of places to eat and drink by the beach.
Bus stop 19 or 20, about 3km (2 miles) east of Koukounaries.

Agia Paraskevi (Ormos Platanias)

With almost 1.5km (1 mile) of clean yellow sand, Agia Paraskevi is the only beach on Skiathos that can really compete with Koukounaries. It is no less busy in high season, and at the west end is one of the poshest hotels on the island, which not only rents

umbrellas but also luxurious beach gazebo tents.
Midway between Koukounaries and Hora.

Vromolimnos

Vromolimnos is the island's youth-oriented, adrenalin-activity beach, boasting waterskiing, wakeboarding, bungee jumping and the rest, as well as the noisiest day-time beach party and after-dark dance scene on Skiathos.
On the west side of the Kanapitsa peninsula, 20 minutes' walk from bus stop 13.

Tzaneria (Porto Nostos)

This attractive curve of pebbly sand is less crowded than its neighbours, and is home to one of the island's better diving centres as well as offering a range of watersports.
Bus stop 12.

SKOPELOS

Skopelos is narrow and mountainous, and its central spine of hills is covered with pine-scented woods, pocket-sized vineyards, and groves of olive, lemon and almond trees.

It's a little larger than its near neighbour Skiathos, but in tourism terms it is still in its sister's shadow – mainly because it has no airport and only a handful of small pebbly coves and bays that for beach lovers cannot match up to Skiathos's golden sands.

But it is still a very alluring island. The wooded slopes beneath its highest point (680m/2,230ft) are criss-crossed by walking paths that are shaded by pine trees and are hilly enough to be challenging but not intimidating to any fit walker. Around a dozen convents and monasteries – most of them deserted – are scattered around the island.

The beaches may be small, but the water is gorgeously clear. Tourism has not completely taken over, with many islanders still making a traditional living from farming and fishing. For those in search of adventure, there are sailing dinghies and motorboats for hire, scuba diving and boat trips to Alonissos and its Marine Park.

Skopelos is around 19km (12 miles) long from its narrow northern tip to its wider southern coast, and is only 8km (5 miles) across at its widest point. Most of the coast northwest of Hora is rocky and inaccessible, and the best beaches are on the west and south coasts.

Skopelos is about 6km (4 miles) east of Skiathos (at its closest point).

Glossa (Loutraki)

Glossa, near the northern tip of Skopelos, sits on a hillside, facing west towards Skiathos. It is Skopelos's second-largest village. Loutraki, its harbour (far below the village), is the first stop for hydrofoils and catamarans from Skiathos, but the service exists mainly for the benefit of islanders. There is no beach here and little reason to disembark.

28km (17 miles) northwest of Hora.

Agios Ioannis

This picturesquely located little monastery church is probably the only reason to visit Glossa. The climactic wedding scene in *Mamma Mia!* was filmed here in 2007. The white chapel, lined with frescoes, perches atop a steep crag 100m (325ft) above the sea, reached by 105 steps.

5km (3 miles) southeast of Glossa on the way to Hora. Open: irregularly, enquire in Glossa.

Hora (Skopelos Town)

The island's main village has great character, with a historic centre full of whitewashed houses with painted wooden balconies and grey stone roofs, overlooked by a cluster of age-old churches.

Hora has expanded since a new and bigger harbour and marina were completed in 2003, and in summer it is ever more popular with Greek holidaymakers from the mainland, who fill the cafés along the harbour, boost a

MAMMA MIA!

When the film of the ABBA musical *Mamma Mia!* premiered in 2008, the travel industry predicted a boom in travel to Skopelos and its neighbours. The cast stayed on Skopelos, which doubled as the fictional island of Kalokeri. The film's link with the island is well promoted, and tunes from the soundtrack play seemingly endlessly in café-bars, and will probably still be heard long after the film is forgotten. After all, *Zorba the Greek* was made in 1964, and its theme tune (by Mikis Theodorakis) is still heard on every Greek island.

lively after-dark scene, and – because they demand authentic Greek food – ensure that the restaurants are a cut above the average.

Hora has its own beach – a stretch of shingle that has been enhanced by tons of sand dredged from the seabed during the building of the new marina – with a café-bar on the sand next to the harbour which offers free sunbeds and parasols to patrons. However, it's not as good as the island's other beaches, which are worth making the effort to seek out even if you're staying in Hora.

Folklore Museum

A short distance from the harbour, follow the signs (from several points on the waterfront) to discover an interesting collection of traditional Skopelot costumes, pottery, embroidery and other arts and crafts.
Tel: (24240) 23494. Open: daily 10.30am–2.30pm & 6–10.30pm.

Moni Evangelistrias

This 18th-century monastery stands on the slopes of Mt Palouki, above Hora. Its magnificent interior, adorned with gilt icons and colourful frescoes, is famed for its icon of the Virgin.
2km (1¼ miles) east of Hora. Tel: (24240) 23230. Open: daily 9am–1pm & 3–5pm. Free admission.

Moni Prodromou

Built in 1721, this monastery features a carved iconostasis and is located to

offer striking views of the town and harbour. It was built in 1721.
Tel: (24240) 22395. Open: daily 8am–1pm & 5–8pm. Free admission.

Panagitsa tou Pirgou

Overlooking the sea above the north side of the harbour, this is the most prominent of scores of churches and chapels tucked away in the steep lanes of the old quarter.
North side of the harbour. Open: dawn until dusk.

Panormos

For those seeking a purpose-built holiday resort on the beach, Panormos is the best option on Skopelos. It is on a west-facing bay (so there are great sunsets) with a main pebbly beach and a series of smaller sandy coves and bays on either side. Canoes, pedalos and small motorboats can be hired, and windsurfing and waterskiing are also on offer.
18km (11 miles) west of Hora.

Stafilos

This pebbly beach on a deep blue bay is the closest really good beach to Hora. It has a few places to eat and drink (some of which are only open in July and August) and in high season it can become very busy.
4km (2½ miles) south of Hora, on the southeast coast.

Velanio

The rocky headland of Cape Stafilos separates this smaller pebble beach from Stafilos. There are few facilities (apart from a summer *cantina* which sells snacks and cold drinks), and it attracts fewer visitors.

About 1km (²/₃ mile) east of Stafilos beach.

Agnontas

Skopelos's third harbour village is Agnontas, on a bay on the south coast. This sleepy little harbour is normally used only by yachts, fishing boats and day-trip boats, but ferries and hydrofoils make occasional stops. It has a handful of bars and tavernas, a minuscule lido, and Limnonari beach is less than 1km (²/₃ mile) away, on the north side of the bay.

About 5km (3 miles) south of Hora.

Limnonari

This south-facing beach has a long sweep of coarse sand and white pebbles, overlooked by steep pine-covered slopes and rocky headlands. The water here is almost always calm and is very clear.

About 6km (4 miles) south of Hora.

ALONISSOS

Alonissos is only a half-hour ferry ride from Skopelos. Tourism is low-key here, and even in high season there are empty stretches of beach separated by rocky headlands and overlooked by steep pine-covered slopes and cliffs where rare falcons roost. The waters around Alonissos are vividly blue and amazingly clear, and the sea around the uninhabited islands to its north has been designated as the National Marine Park of Alonissos – one of the largest nature reserves in Europe, and a refuge for the endangered monk seal, dolphins and other creatures.

There are only two villages of any size, plus a scattering of tiny hamlets around the coast, and many of the most attractive beaches are hard to get to except on foot or by boat.

In 1965 an earthquake rocked Alonissos's main village, which is now known as Paleo Horio ('Old Village'), and most islanders moved to new homes at Patitiri. Mt Geladias, at 456m (1,496ft), is the island's highest point, and its flanks are traversed by a network of waymarked walking paths. With thick pine woods to give shade and the sea never more than 10–15 minutes' walk away for a quick dip, this makes Alonissos a favourite island for walkers. It also offers opportunities for divers, with wall, cave and wreck dives.

Patitiri

Purpose-built to rehouse homeless islanders after the 1965 earthquake, Patitiri is a surprisingly lively and welcoming little village. Streets of boxy little houses (their lines softened by great clumps of bougainvillea and pot plants) rise above a harbour where ferries from Skopelos and Skiathos call, a rocky beach and a taverna-lined quayside. There is no public transport on Alonissos; instead, a fleet of taxis shuttles continuously back and forth between Patitiri, Paleo Horio and other points. You can also call taxis from your hotel or from any taverna, but at busy times they may take some time to arrive. Patitiri may seem to be an out-of-the-way place, but it has moved with the times – the whole village has free Wi-Fi, so if you are travelling with a laptop you can check your email while sitting in a café.

A rocky promontory jutting into the sea separates Patitiri harbour from Votsi, less than 1km (²⁄₃ mile) to the north, which also has a small harbour full of yachts and fishing boats. Inland, along the main road, the two villages have virtually merged, turning Votsi into a suburb of Patitiri.

Alonissos History Museum

This well-designed little museum houses a fearsome collection of flintlocks, pistols, daggers, cutlasses and other relics of the island's piratical past, maps and documents relating to Greece's struggle for independence, and a fascinating exhibition of peasant costumes and old-fashioned farming equipment. It also has a rooftop café. *200m (220yds) south of and uphill from the harbour, signposted. Open: May & Sept daily 11am–9pm, Jun–Aug daily 11am–7pm.*

National Marine Park of Alonissos

A variety of boats leave every day in summer for the waters of the National

A view across the port of Patitiri

Marine Park. You would be extremely lucky to see one of the very rare monk seals which breed in the sea-caves of some of the uninhabited islands protected by the park, including Gioura, 25km (16 miles) north of Alonissos. This rocky isle, according to Homer, was the home of the Cyclopes, the man-eating, one-eyed giants that attacked Odysseus and his crew on their way home from the Trojan War. There is a much better chance of seeing rare Eleonora's falcons diving over the island cliffs where they nest. Boats also pause at the island's famous 'blue grotto' and anchor for lunch and a visit to a tiny, picturesque monastery at Kira Panagia island before returning to Patitiri.

Morning departures from Patitiri harbour. Book with Ikos Travel (tel: (24240) 65320; www.ikostravel.com) or Planitis Marine Park Cruises (tel: (24240) 65288; www.alonnisostravel.gr).

Paleo Horio

As villagers moved out of Paleo Horio, foreigners (and mainland Greeks) moved in, rebuilding battered old houses into second homes, craft workshops and artists' studios. The main street is lined with cafés and shops selling handmade toys, ceramics, paintings and textiles that are of a higher quality and more attractive than run-of-the-mill tourist tat, and there are great views on all sides.

Traditional House Museum

Standing above the church at the end of Paleo Horio main street, this family home has been lovingly restored, with old-fashioned household utensils and furniture, family portraits and photographs. A plaque on the wall outside commemorates the nine villagers murdered by German troops on 15 August 1944.

Platea Iroon. Open: May–Oct daily 10am–6pm. Admission charge.

Milia and Hrisi Milia

Alonissos has few sandy beaches. Hrisi Milia is one of the best, and is easy to get to from Patitiri. A headland separates it from Milia, to the south, a smaller white-pebble beach on a pretty bay with a small summer *cantina* serving snacks and drinks.

About 4km (2½ miles) north of Patitiri.

Megalos and Mikros Mourtias

These two beaches are side by side on the south coast of the island, about half an hour's walk from Paleo Horio. Both beaches are pebbly, but the sea bottom is sandier, the water is very clean and there are several beach tavernas among the olive groves.

Steni Vala and Kalamakia

The tiny village of Steni Vala is set on the north shore of a narrow inlet that provides a fine natural harbour and was once a pirates' haven. Yachts and fishing boats moor along a quayside with a row of tavernas that do a good line in fresh fish (islanders come from Patitiri for lunch or dinner). Kalamakia, about 3km north of Steni Vala, also has a handful of good seafood restaurants and a small pebbly beach.

About 10–13km (6–7 miles) north of Patitiri.

Agios Dimitrios

Saving the best until last, Agios Dimitrios is the largest and least crowded beach on the east coast of Alonissos. Its sweep of clean pebbles looks out towards the almost uninhabited island of Peristera, across a narrow strait through which yachts and cruisers sail on their way to the National Marine Park. Loungers and parasols are provided for patrons of two small tavernas at the southern end of the beach, but the rest is usually virtually deserted.

SKIROS (Skyros)

Skiros is an island apart. It lies way off to the south and east of its neighbours (though on a clear day it can be seen from Alonissos). It is roughly hourglass-shaped, and north of its narrow waist the pretty main village looks out to sea and downward to pine woods, pastures and a coastline fringed with long shingle beaches. The southern half of the island is strikingly different – a jagged lunar landscape of shattered boulders where even goats have a tough time grazing. Skiros has a strong handicrafts heritage that features beaten-copper dishes and bowls, decorated ceramics, embroidery and elaborately carved wooden furniture. Village homes open straight onto the street, and a walk through Hora's steep lanes allows glimpses into house-proud parlours, decorated and furnished with

A jumble of flat-roofed houses in Skiros Town

local products. Ferry services between Skiros and Skiathos are, literally, sporadic; the easiest way to get here is by sea from Kimi on Evia, or by air direct from Athens.

24km (15 miles) northeast of Kimi on the east coast of Evia.

Hora (Skiros Town)

Hora is a spectacularly pretty agglomeration of flat-roofed, whitewashed houses which cover a hilltop beneath the crumbling ruins of a 1,000-year-old Byzantine fortress. It is still an idyllically old-fashioned community, though the generation of older people who clung to traditional costume until the 1990s has passed on, and a few smart café-bars and hotels – catering mainly to Greek summer visitors – have made an appearance. Hora is truly a three-dimensional puzzle; it is easy to wander for some time through this labyrinth of lanes and alleys before finally emerging at the gateway to the ancient castle, but the puzzle is worth solving to catch the sunset from this highest point in the village.

Kastro and Agios Georgios

An arched gateway below the castle ramparts leads inside and to the monastery of Agios Georgios, inside the castle walls, which occupies the highest point of the castle. It contains remarkable frescoes of Christ Pantocrator, but it was severely damaged by an earthquake in 2001 and has not yet fully reopened, although the lower part

SKIROS PONIES

Skiros is famous for a unique breed of miniature pony. Indigenous to the island for at least 1,200 years, the ponies were once used in the rocky fields but were supplanted first by donkeys, then by machinery. Left to fend for themselves, the number of pure-bred Skiros ponies has now dropped to about 100, but there are hopes that a breeding programme will save this little horse from extinction.

of the building can sometimes be visited. Access to parts of the castle is also limited because of earthquake damage.
Kastro. Open: irregularly, several times weekly.

Manos Faltaits Museum

Founded in 1964, this fascinating collection is housed in the founder's family mansion and contains a plethora of island arts and crafts, textiles, pottery, paintings, woodwork and metalwork. It was one of the first museums in Greece to celebrate the lives and work of ordinary islanders (rather than the glories of the ancient world) and since then has spawned many imitators, few of which can match the depth and breadth of its collection.
Paleopirgo, Hora. Tel: (22220) 91232; www.faltaits.gr. Open: daily 9am–1.30pm & 5–8.30pm. Admission charge.

Magazia (Molos)

This long, east-facing sandy beach within sight of Hora has grown into a flourishing small resort with an adequate assortment of places to stay, sleep and eat

RUPERT BROOKE

Just off the main street in Hora, a bronze statue of a nude male youth (symbolising poetry) commemorates the English war poet Rupert Brooke (1887–1915), buried on Skiros after he died of typhus aboard a hospital ship at Moudros. When the statue was unveiled, its nudity shocked villagers, who draped it in sheets for the sake of decency. Brooke's grave – in his own words, the 'corner of a foreign field that is forever England' – is in an isolated olive grove, overlooking Treis Boukes bay in southern Skiros, 23km (14 miles) from Linaria. It's very hard to find, and unless you're a real lover of his work it's hardly worth the journey.

(though most people prefer to stay in or near Hora and visit the beach during the day), and it avoids the excesses of some better-known islands.

1km (²⁄₃ mile) northeast of Hora.

EVIA (Euboea)

Greece's second-largest island hardly qualifies as an island at all. The Gulf of Evia, which separates it from the mainland, is only 100m (328ft) wide at its narrowest point, and is crossed by a road bridge (which can be retracted to allow ships to use the channel). In many ways, Evia feels like a part of mainland Greece, but explorers who take time to discover its charms will not go away disappointed.

Since the opening of Athens' new international airport, which is little more than an hour's drive away, Evia has become very accessible year-round, making it ideal for a holiday in early spring or late autumn, when charter flights do not operate. It has plenty of beaches, some sandy, some pebbly, and many of them have hardly been touched by tourism (though those on the southwest coast, closest to the mainland, are often packed with Greek holidaymakers on summer weekends). In the north it has several natural thermal spas and several resorts that

The Venetian-Greek church of Agia Paraskevi stands in the middle of Halkida

specialise in therapeutic breaks. Inland, fertile valleys and thickly wooded hills cloaked in plane and chestnut trees contrast with rugged hills that can offer challenging walking. In ancient times, Evia was a powerful state in its own right, while after the Venetian conquest it was one of the jewels in Venice's Aegean crown and was known as Negroponte. It fell to the Turks in 1470, and there are ancient Venetian and Turkish relics dotted around its coast and countryside.

Halkida

Few people linger in the island's capital, which was important in antiquity but is today an uninspiring industrial and commercial centre. Its only points of interest (apart from the 'Sliding Bridge' connecting it to the mainland) are a minor natural wonder and a lumpen Turkish fortress.

Eretria

The ancient city-state of Eretria was a powerful ally of Athens, but most of its remains are now buried beneath the modern village of the same name. The remains of an ancient theatre, sanctuary and gymnasium can be seen northwest of the village centre, and a small archaeological museum contains pottery and bronzes discovered on the site of the ancient city.

Eretria is 21km (13 miles) southeast of Halkida. Theatre and museum are signposted. Tel: (22210) 62206. Open: Tue–Sun 8.30am–3pm. Combined admission charge to museum and site.

Evripou

The current which swirls through the narrow channel between Halkida and the mainland changes direction quite dramatically several times daily, creating a whirlpool effect. In the

The stone battlements of Castello Rosso loom over Karistos harbour

almost tideless Aegean, this is a puzzle that defied even the mighty intellect of Aristotle (who is said to have plunged into it in frustration) and has still not been fully explained.

Town centre, visible from bridge (timing unpredictable, patience required!).

Karababa Fortress (Frourio Karababas)

Built by a Turkish bey to control the strategic narrows of the Evoikos Kolpos (Gulf of Evia), this is no fairy-tale castle but a grimly efficient fort, sited so that its guns could fire with maximum effect on any would-be invader.

On a hilltop north of the main road at the east side of the Evripou bridge. Tel: (22290) 62206. Open: Mon–Sat 8.30am–3pm. Free admission.

Karistos

With shuttle ferries connecting it with Rafina on the mainland (only 30 minutes from Athens airport), this is a much more prepossessing gateway to Evia than Halkida. It stands on a broad south-facing bay, and behind it is a wild hinterland dominated by 1,398m (4,660ft) Mt Ohi. There is a long, sand-and-shingle beach west of town, but like most gateway ports the rest of the island beckons.

Close to the southern tip of Evia, 90km (56 miles) southeast of Halkida.

Kastro (Castello Rosso)

The Venetian 'red castle', dating from the 13th century, looms above the town. Like Karababa, it is more functional than decorative, but its huge empty shell with red sandstone battlements and bastions is very impressive.

1.5km (1 mile) from Karistos harbour. Open daily. Free admission.

Kimi

This small fishing and farming village (and ferry port from where boats leave for Skiros) overlooking a bay on the east coast of Evia is the most attractive village on the island, with an array of old red-roofed houses, good tavernas and pebbly beaches south of town on Ormos Kipis (Kipi Bay). Inland lies Evia's highest mountain massif, Dirfis, rising to 1,743m (5,700ft) above sea level.

Midway along the east coast.

MONK SEALS

There are fewer than 500 monk seals left in the world, and almost half of them live in Greek waters, with around 50 in the Alonissos National Marine Park. In the past they were hunted for food and for their skins, which were used to make the traditional curly-toed sandals worn by islanders on Alonissos and Skiros. They are no longer hunted, and the main threat to their survival is now loss of habitat and depletion of their food supplies by overfishing. A few pups are born each year in the sea-caves around Alonissos, and as monk seals can live for 45 years the population is slowly growing. They also breed on deserted Poliaigios in the Cyclades and on Saria in the Dodecanese. The Hellenic Society for the Study and Protection of the Monk Seal (MOm) monitors the seals and campaigns for their protection. To find out how to support these efforts – or to 'adopt' a seal – visit *www.mom.gr*

Getting away from it all

Greece's most popular islands are, of course, those which are easiest to get to. But tantalisingly close to islands with international airports, bustling resorts or on main ferry routes lie dozens more. For independent-minded travellers, these can be surprisingly easy to get to in summer, with hydrofoils and small ferries linking them with their larger neighbours. The mainland also lies within sight of many islands, and it's easy to combine an island holiday with a couple of days' visit.

THE MAINLAND

Athens, with its world-class museums and archaeological sites, historic centre and tempting shopping streets, is within day-trip distance of Aigina, Angistri, Poros and Idra in the Saronic isles. From Poros – only five minutes by boat from Methana on the mainland – you can make a one-day trip (using a rented car) to ancient sites that span millennia of Greek history, including Epidavros, Corinth and ancient Mycenae (Mikines). Evia, with a road bridge connecting it to the mainland, is a good base for visits that can include Athens, ancient Delphi, or the cliff-top monasteries of the Meteora in Thessaly. From Thassos, it's a short hop to the historic port of Kavala and the outstanding Roman ruins of Filipi. From Zakinthos, you can take a ferry to Kilini, then catch a bus or drive to ancient Olympia, birthplace of the Games. From Corfu, take a ferry to Igoumenitsa, then travel by road to Ioannina on its emerald-green lake and onward into the breathtaking Pindos mountains of northern Epirus.

THE SMALLER ISLANDS

Scattered among the bigger, better-known islands are many tinier isles, some with thriving villages, some deserted but for a handful of fishermen. These dots on the map are not always remote in terms of distance. Many are within an hour's sailing of popular resorts and international airports. But reaching them can be a challenge, and it is surprising how crowded some of them can be in high season. Most have one village and a single small beach, and space can be limited in July and August.

Outside the peak months, however, the small isles are a delight for real island fans. If you can be content with a beach, a book and a simple dinner in an unsophisticated taverna, they offer a sense of peace and isolation – the Greeks call it *isikhia* – that the developed resorts cannot match.

Craft of all sorts ply the blue seas of the Greek islands

Agathonissi, Arki and Lipsi

These three islands, with scores of uninhabited rocks and skerries, form a lovely mini-archipelago in the northern Dodecanese, sheltered from northerly winds by Samos and the Turkish coast.

Agathonissi

A long, low, barren isle of fishermen and goatherds, its name means 'thorny island'. Around 150 people live here, and the main village, sheltered among low hills, is simply called Megalo Horio – 'the big village' – to distinguish it from the even tinier Mikro Horio. *30km (19 miles) east of Patmos. Weekly ferries from Patmos and Samos (Pithagorio).*

Arki

Arki, with a population of fewer than 70, lies in the midst of a jumble of even tinier rocks, and on a clear day, with the hills of Patmos, Ikaria, Samos, Turkey and the smaller islands nearby ringing the horizon, it seems to be afloat on an inland lake instead of in the open sea. Its attractions are: superbly clear water, excellent snorkelling and lots of islets on which to sunbathe and picnic. *10km (6 miles) east of Patmos. Weekly ferries from Patmos and Samos (Pithagorio).*

Lipsi

Almost 600 people live on Lipsi, making it the metropolis of this mini-island group. Half a dozen tiny white churches, each with its distinctive blue dome, stand out against the hillside terraces which make the most of each patch of fertile land. The broad harbour is home to a small fishing fleet, and with its shallow, glass-clear water it is a natural aquarium full of colourful fish and other Aegean sea life. A sandy beach, five minutes' walk north of the harbour, is complemented by white sand coves along the north shore. *8km (5 miles) east of Patmos; weekly ferries and frequent excursion boats (summer only).*

Agios Efstratios

One of Greece's genuinely remote islands where political prisoners used to be exiled, Agios Efstratios lies almost exactly in the centre of the northeast Aegean. Empty horizons on all sides add to the sense of isolation. Its sole village was built to rehouse islanders after an earthquake in 1967, and owners of its identical houses have gradually added individual touches: flowers, vine arbours and other features. The harbour is so small that large ferries cannot dock and passengers are taken ashore by dinghy.

There are small swimming coves on the east coast. *40km (25 miles) south of Limnos, served by ferries between Limnos and Rafina on the mainland.*

Anafi

Saucepan-shaped Anafi has steep sea cliffs, a high and arid hinterland, around 300 inhabitants and no cars. Almost all the islanders live in the small port of Agios Nikolaos, on the south coast, or in Hora, on the hill immediately above it. Anafi's beach is at Klisidhi, on the south coast. *One hour east of Santorini; infrequent ferries.*

Halki

Like its neighbours Simi and Tilos (*see p155*), Halki belongs to the southern Dodecanese, is within easy reach of Rhodes and has become a resort island in its own right. Its

Lipsi's hillsides are dotted with blue domes

harbour village, Emporeio, is very pretty, with fine old houses. Some of these delightful three-storey mansions, with their peeling stucco façades and drooping balconies, are being restored as guesthouses.

50km (31 miles) from Rhodes. Daily ferries (from Kamiros Skala); frequent hydrofoils (from Rhodes Town).

Horio

Halki's medieval village is now a ghost town, with a dilapidated watchtower of the Knights of St John. The walk is rewarded by a fine view of Rhodes (*see pp106–11*).

3km (2 miles) west of Emborios.

Fourni

This barren, hilly island with its scalloped coastline is named after the old-fashioned outdoor bread ovens (*fourni*), still used in a few villages, which its twin hills resemble from a distance. Its small, peaceful harbour village is spectacularly sited on a glorious west-facing bay.

18km (11 miles) east of Ikaria, served by frequent Pireas–Ikaria–Samos ferries.

Kastelorizo (Megisti)

Greece's most remote island lies within a few hundred metres of the Turkish coast. In the 19th century, it was an important trading port, but it went into a decline after its seizure by Italy in 1912. Before World War II, its harbour was a stop on Italian and French flying-boat routes to the

Middle East. From 16,000 people a century ago, there are only 200 now. Despite its ghost-town atmosphere and lack of beaches, it is a delightful island, with fantastic snorkelling around its rocky shores.

105km (65 miles) east of Rhodes; weekly ferries and flights from Rhodes.

Kimolos

This tiny island is one of the Aegean's great undiscovered destinations.

1.5km (1 mile) from Milos.

Hora (Kimolos Town)

The island's main village is a clutter of white hillside houses backed by six windmills.

In the middle of the island, 1km (²⁄₃ mile) from Psathi.

Paleokastro

The battlements of a ruined Venetian fortress surround the island's oldest church, the whitewashed Hristos chapel.

2km (1¼ miles) northwest of Kimolos Town. Free admission.

Kithnos

Most visitors bypass gentle Kithnos – the first stop on the ferry route from Pireas to the western Cyclades – en route to better-known isles further south, and it is hard to argue that they are missing much.

Kithnos has little to offer by way of beaches or sightseeing, and its landscapes are less dramatic than many of its neighbours.

Dryopida

Stucco-walled homes with red-tiled roofs make this farming village – the island's capital in medieval times – look more Italian than Cycladic.

5km (3 miles) south of Kithnos Town.

Hora (Kithnos Town)

The remaining traditional buildings of the village are dwarfed by new construction.

Centre of the island.

Kefalos (Akr Kefalos)

The ruins of a medieval Venetian castle crown the north-facing headland.

North tip of the island, 7km (4 miles) from Kithnos Town. Free admission.

Metamorphosis (Church of the Transfiguration)

An interesting 17th-century church.

Village centre. Open: daily. Free admission.

Spilaio Katafigi (Cave of Refuge)

In the middle of the village, the locally famous cave once provided islanders with shelter from pirate raids.

Free admission.

Koufonissia

The Koufonissia are four inhabited islands, surrounded by several more deserted isles, lying south of Naxos.

Donoussa

Solitude is the only real attraction of this near-deserted island, and with more people seeking it each year it is an increasingly scarce commodity. The population of the only village is fewer than 100 and facilities are primitive.

60km (37 miles) east of Naxos Town. Infrequent ferries.

Iraklia

The biggest of the Koufonissia offers a harbour-village set on a scenic bay and walks over rough hillsides to Panagia, its deserted medieval Hora.

25km (16 miles) south of Naxos Town. Daily ferries.

Shinoussa

Like Donoussa, Shinoussa is for those in search of peace and quiet, and, as on Donoussa, more arrive each year, overstretching the island's ability to cater for them.

30km (19 miles) southeast of Naxos Town. Daily ferries.

Psara

Rocky, eerie Psara has a special place in the hearts of Greeks. During the War of Independence, this tiny northeast Aegean isle added its fleet of armed merchant ships to the rebel Greek fleet. In 1824, the Turks landed and massacred most of its inhabitants. The few survivors left the island, which then remained uninhabited from 1824–34. Even today, its population numbers a mere 460 islanders. There is a choice of beaches, with solitude guaranteed.

56km (35 miles) northwest of Hios Town, from where a ferry runs four times a week.

Simi

Tiny Simi retains its delightful serenity, despite a daily invasion of excursionists from Rhodes. In the evening, the island reverts to its natural calm.
27km (17 miles) northwest of Rhodes Town.

Gialos

Gialos is a ghost town with a pleasant air of faded elegance. Around its deep harbour are ranks of tall, elegantly proportioned neoclassical mansions. Most are mere shells, but many are now being restored, as are the windmills above the harbour.

Boatbuilding still goes on at the small yard on the bay.
North coast of Simi.

Moni Panormitis (Panormitis Monastery)

The 18th-century monastery has a striking carved icon in its small chapel and a mock-Baroque *campanile* dating from 1905.
15km (9 miles) south of Gialos. Tel: (22460) 71354. Open: daily 7am–2pm & 3–8pm. Donation expected.

Pedion

Pedion is situated on a horseshoe-shaped bay with a sandy bottom and warm water. It is popular with visiting yachts and its pebbly, tree-lined beach is upgraded each summer with imported truckloads of sand.
2km (1¹/₄ miles) east of Gialos on the north coast.

Tilos

Blessed with plentiful springs, Tilos abounds with small, fertile valleys and patches of farmland which provide a contrast to the barren scenery of its hills.
65km (40 miles) west of Rhodes Town.

Livadia

The main village on the island is a pleasant settlement. On a wide, hill-girt bay, it has a long, pebbly beach.
East coast of Tilos.

Megalo Horio

This hilltop village overlooks a patchwork of green cultivation. A battlemented fortress of the Knights of St John lends historic interest. Satellite watchtowers of this fortress are scattered on hills around the island.
7km (4¹/₂ miles) northwest of Livadia. Fortress and watchtowers freely accessible.

Mikro Horio

Deserted since the 1950s, this ghost village makes a fine destination for a lovely walk from Livadia, with rewarding views from its castle keep.
2km (1¹/₄ miles) west of Livadia. Castle: free admission.

Sponges are a popular island souvenir

Shopping

There are bargains to be found, though perhaps not where you would expect. Souvenir shops in resorts from Corfu to Rhodes sell much the same range of slogan T-shirts and brightly coloured imported leisurewear. For more authentic mementoes of your trip, look in the laiki *– the municipal street market in larger island villages and towns – for items such as brass goat bells, shepherds' wooden walking sticks or tiny Greek coffee cups.*

Contrary to popular tourist belief, haggling over prices is not the norm, though the price of everything does drop outside peak tourist season.

Shops traditionally open between 9am and 2pm, close until around 6pm and reopen until about 9pm, though in major resorts many shops catering to tourists stay open all afternoon and late into the night. Most shops, except those in resort areas, close on Sunday.

Value added tax at 23 per cent is charged on anything you buy, although a lower rate of 6.5 per cent currently applies to accommodation. Tax-free shopping is available to visitors from outside the European Union at selected shops in the most popular holiday isles. The Hellenic Duty Free Shops chain operates duty-free shops for passengers leaving from most airports.

WHAT TO BUY
Antiquities
You need an export permit to take real antiques or icons out of Greece. This is rarely granted, and genuine antiquities are, in any case, very scarce. Beware of fakes, as they are so well made that it is hard to distinguish them from originals. Archaeological museums in Greece license a range of attractive replicas, for example of the enigmatic statues of the Cycladic civilisation, that are a much better buy.

Beads and bangles
Brightly coloured ceramic beads, necklaces, gold- and silver-plated bracelets and the black and blue glass beads traditionally believed to ward off evil make cheap and cheerful gifts. *Komboloi* or 'worry-beads', carried by many island men, are sold very cheaply at street kiosks and in souvenir shops.

Clothing
Good buys include cotton-knit sweaters and, on more fashionable islands such as Mikonos, Santorini or Paros, a wide range of attractive and imaginative summerwear by young Greek designers.

Cotton and linen prints, silks and cotton knits are popular.

Footwear

Boots and shoes are well made and affordable. In markets on Crete you will find old-fashioned cobblers selling Cretan riding boots. Sandals sold in tourist markets rarely wear well, but on Skiros you can buy the unique, hard-wearing sandals worn by islanders, which are soled with slices of old car tyre. Main street stores in Rhodes Town are a good bet for classic leather shoes at prices well below the European average.

Jewellery

Jewellers abound in small island towns as well as in big resorts. Traditional designs include a variety of good-luck charms, while on Mikonos, Paros, Naxos, Santorini and other islands you will find craftsmen working to both modern interpretations and ancient designs. Silver jewellery is cheaper, but gold can be more expensive than elsewhere in Europe.

Lace and embroidery

Traditionally made lace napkins and tablecloths are excellent buys in Corfu Town and in Rhodes, but beware of cheap, machine-made imitations.

Leather goods

Leather handbags, satchels and travel bags made solely for the tourist trade are sold in markets wherever holiday-makers go. Prices are low, and this is one area where you may haggle. Workmanship is not always first-rate. Examine seams and straps before buying.

WHERE TO SHOP
Markets

The local *laiki* market in large island towns sells produce, hardware and everyday goods and, with piles of vivid fruit and vegetables, it offers lots of photo opportunities and an insight into local lifestyles, as well as a chance to buy quirky mementoes of your trip.

The *laiki* takes place on weekday mornings and is a great place to stock up on fresh fruit, cheeses and vegetables for picnics or for self-catering. Here, too, you'll find longer-lasting island specialities such as dried and candied fruit, nuts, sunflower and pumpkin seeds, island honey and aromatic herbs. Hours vary seasonally: ask for local

Jars of goodies in Thassos Town

times at the *dimarcheio* (town hall), island tourist office or your hotel.

More formal shopping is patchy and depends very much on the island's holiday clientele: fashionable islands such as Mikonos have designer boutiques to compare with the best in Europe; smaller, simpler islands have smaller, simpler shops.

The best island markets for shopping and picture-taking are listed here, together with a sample of other shops.

Corfu

Jewellery in silver and in 18- and 20- to 22-carat gold can be found in a row of quality jewellers along the Liston arcades behind the Spianada (*see p26*). A fine choice of island handicrafts can be found in all major resorts.

Corfu Town

Corfu Fine Jewellery Corfu Fine Jewellery sells handmade silver and 14- and 18-carat gold pieces in Byzantine style, including necklaces, chains, rings and earrings.
Filellinon 16, Corfu Town.
Tel: (26610) 39054.
Corfu Leather Market Corfu Leather Market specialises in handmade leather clothes, bags and other accessories for men and women.
Dona and Nikos Theotoki 7,
Corfu Town. Tel: (26610) 21297.

Kassiopi

Aleka's Lace House Aleka's is one of the best places to buy the embroidery,

weaving, pillow lace and crochet for which Corfu is famous.
Kassiopi. Tel: (26630) 81402.

Crete
Iraklio

Dimotiki Agora (Municipal Market)
A fine market where self-caterers can shop for local products such as cheese, olives, herbs and other ingredients, and buy typical Cretan woven shepherds' bags and curly wooden walking sticks to take home.
Odos 1866.

Hania

Dimotiki Agora (Municipal Market)
Hania's covered market is a great place to find local produce and Cretan souvenirs. The narrow lanes between the market area and Odos Halidon are stuffed with shops selling hand-made Cretan riding boots, sandals and bags.
Nikoforou Foka.
Kreta Gold Kreta Gold has been selling quality work by some of Greece's finest goldsmiths in Hania for more than 30 years.
Old Harbour. Tel: (28210) 42623;
www.kretagold.com

Hios

Mastiha Shop Sweets, desserts, and liqueurs made from Hios's famous *mastiha* tree. Also has branches in Iraklio (Crete) and Lafkada.
Leoforos Aegeou 36, Hora. Tel: (22710)
31600. www.mastihashop.com

Shopping in Corfu Town

Lesvos

In Mitilini, Odos Ermou, which runs north–south as far as the castle walls (*see p124*), is lined with dusty antique shops selling everything from rusting scimitars and flintlock pistols to tarnished brass and silverware and engravings of island scenes. In Molivos, you'll find a number of imaginative souvenir stores.

Mikonos
Delos Dolphins

Established in 1985, Delos Dolphins sells classic handmade Greek jewellery in gold and silver.
Hora. Tel: (22890) 22765.

Gofas Jewellery

This is the Mikonos branch of the well-known Athens jeweller and sells high-quality, attractively designed works in gold and silver, and precious stones.
Hora. Tel: (22890) 24521.

Ilias Lalaounis Creations

Pieces inspired by a 4,000-year-old tradition in Greek gold jewellery-making, combining ancient skills and modern techniques.
Polykandrioti 14, Hora.
Tel: (22890) 22444.

Turquoise Art Studio

This studio sells works of art made from natural materials and ceramics.
Tourlianis 6, Hora. Tel: (22890) 28835.

Rhodes

Odos Sokratous, the shopping thoroughfare of the Old Town (*see pp110–11*), is packed with fine jewellery and leatherware stores. More jewellers plus shoe stores and designer boutiques are to be found on and around Odos Venizelou, in the heart of the New Town. Lambraki, in the New Town, is also a good bet for designer wear.

Hellenic Fine Art and Jewellery

A one-stop shop for all your souvenirs and gifts.
Aristotelous 17, Rhodes Old Town.
Tel: (22410) 39492.

JLo by Jennifer Lopez

Daywear, evening wear, shoes and accessories for disco queens.
Sofoklis Verrizelon 100.
Tel: (22410) 21033.

Santorini
Mamayoma Art

This shop sells a very wide selection of museum-grade copies of works of art spanning some 4,000 years of Greek culture, from jewellery to frescoes, sculpture and ceramics.
Oia. Tel: (22860) 71657.

Entertainment

Entertainment in the Greek islands embraces everything from traditional festivals, folk music and dance, to modern ballet, experimental theatre and live performances by international artists in every musical field from Bach and Beethoven to rock and roll.

Many islands host month-long summer art festivals at which the best of Greek artists and international guest performers can be seen and heard, and which offer excellent value for money.

Often these take place within the walls of medieval fortresses or on the stages of 2,000-year-old open-air theatres whose acoustics are still as startlingly clear as when they were built.

The daily English-language *Athens News* and the weekly *Greek News*, which are available from newsstands on most resort islands, list upcoming festivals and other performances on their events pages.

The Greek National Tourist Office also provides lists of events planned for each year, and information on times, ticket prices and reservations is listed locally by island tourist offices (*see p188*).

CINEMAS

A few larger island towns have cinemas, usually old-fashioned and often open-air, where you can catch recently released US and European films with the original soundtrack and Greek subtitles. Posters around town and outside the cinema will tell you what's on and what's on the way.

CULTURAL EVENTS

Annual cultural events usually take place in July to September, and may include modern and ancient drama, classical and ethnic music and dance.

Lesvos

July–August

Summer programme of drama and Greek musical performances in the medieval castles at Molivos and Mytilini. *Tourist Office for the North Aegean, North Aegean Building, Mytilini, Lesvos. Tel: (22510) 42511.*

Paxos

Paxos International Music Festivals

June and September

Contemporary music festival in June; classical, choral and chamber music festival in September.

Municipality of Paxi. Tel: (26620) 32100.
www.paxosfestival.org.uk

Skiathos
Aegean Festival
August–September
Festival of music and dance, held for the first time in 1994, featuring Greek and international performers.
Bourtzi Theatre, Skiathos.
Tel: (24270) 22022.

Thassos
Philippi and Thassos Festival
July–August
Combined programme of dramatic performances held in the ancient theatre at Limenas (*see p128*) and at Philippi on the mainland.
Limenas, Thassos. Tickets and information: Billias Travel Service, Pavlou Mela 37, Limenas. Tel: (25930) 24003.

Santorini (Thira)
International Music Festival of Santorini
August–September
Festival of music and arts held in a modern venue in the island's picturesque capital.
Nomicos Conference Centre, Thira, Santorini. Tel: (22860) 22220.

DANCING
Greek islanders, young and old, have not lost the habit of making their own amusement. Even in clubs patronised by smart young things from Athens, an evening spent dancing to the latest electronic beat may well end in the small hours with a traditional *sirtos*.

You can sample the traditional entertainment island Greeks enjoy at any *exochiko kentro* ('country centre').

Entertainment

The bouzouki is a mainstay of Greek music

These can be some distance from the town or village and their clientele is often holidaying Greek expats.

One of the best places to see traditional island dances is in Rhodes, where the Nelly Dimoglou troupe of dancers performs at the **Ancient Theatre of Rhodes** (*tel: (22410) 20157*) every night from May to October.

NIGHTLIFE

Tourism has combined with the Greek love of dancing to ensure that every island resort has an oversupply of discos and dance clubs. Even tiny villages may have two or three, often in the open air. These start to warm up well after midnight and play an eclectic mix of the latest dance hits and rock oldies, often staying open until dawn in defiance of a patchily enforced rule that they should close at 2am. Many are no more than a dance floor, bar and sound system overlooking the beach, and many survive no more than one or two summers before reopening with a different management and DJ. It is therefore difficult to make hard and fast recommendations.

In any case, there is little to choose between them, except for the DJ's taste in tracks. Admission is usually free, but drinks are two to three times as expensive as in an ordinary bar.

Islands with a long-standing name for bop-till-you-drop nightlife include Corfu, Ios, Paros and Mikonos, but it is a quiet island indeed that does not have a nightspot and dance venue.

Corfu

Kavos is Corfu's nightlife paradise, with more than 80 bars and clubs along its beach and long main street. Venues come and go, but key players include **Futures & Atlantis**; **Limelights**; **Venue**; and the enormous **Stadium Club**. For events and DJs, see *www.eliteproductions.co.uk* or *www.clubbing-in-heaven.co.uk*

Ios
Aftershock

Opened in 2002, Aftershock has established itself as Ios's hottest club, with international DJs spinning house, trance, dance and Athens club tracks. *Main road, Hora. Tel: (3093) 893 0368 (mobile).*

Ios Club

One of the longest-established clubs in the islands plays classical music at sunset and dance music until the early hours. *Hora. Tel: (69765) 18839; www.iosclub.gr*

Kos
Starlight Club

With events by the likes of Hedkandi and Judge Jules, and foam parties every Saturday night, this is the biggest and liveliest club on Kos. *Kardamena. Tel: (22420) 92456; www.starlightclub.gr*

Mikonos
Skandinavian Bar Disco

Mikonos's bawdiest bar-disco near the harbour has been a crowd-pleaser for decades.

Agios Ioannis Barkia, Hora.
Tel: (22890) 22669;
www.skandinavianbar.com

Space

The biggest dance venue on Mikonos plays non-stop techno until the early hours to an audience of 1,000 people.
Plateia Lakkas, Hora. Tel: (22890) 24100;
www.spacemykonos.com

Rhodes

The Sting Club

Greek DJs plus the latest sounds make this Faliraki's hottest club.
Coast Road, Faliraki. Tel: (22410) 86891;
www.stingclub.com

Zakinthos

Factory

Factory attracts dance scene pilgrims with great cocktails, theme nights and special events, and wide-screen TV.
Argassi. Tel: 26950 74398;
www.djgogos.gr

Rescue

With space for 2,000 people, five bars (two outside) and top imported DJs, Rescue is Laganas's nightlife landmark.
Laganas beach. Tel: 09697 260 03387 (mobile); www.rescueclub.net

Zeros

Top-quality sounds and DJs, also famous for its theme parties.
Laganas beach. Tel: (26950) 53326;
www.zerosclubzante.com

FESTIVALS

Religious festivals in the Greek islands combine solemn ritual with merry-making, feasting, drinking and dancing. The most important events of the island year are also times of family reunion.

Easter

This is celebrated according to the Orthodox calendar throughout Greece, with feasting on lamb and goat, usually barbecued on the spit outdoors, on Easter Sunday, followed by midnight Mass.

Koimisis tis Theotokou (Assumption of the Virgin) *15 August* Celebrated on all islands with feasting and dancing (Paniyiria). Special pilgrimages and processions are held at Markopoulo on Kefalonia, on Skiathos and on Tinos.

TELEVISION

National TV channels include the state-owned ET1, NET, ET3 and ERT Digital. Privately owned channels include Alpha, Alter, ANT1, Mega, Skai and Star. All the main channels broadcast numerous imported English-language programming, subtitled into Greek. Most large hotels offer a limited choice of satellite TV channels. Pay-TV offerings include Cartoon Network, Nova, Boomerang, Disney Channel, Fox Life and National Geographic. There are also around 40 small regional stations based in the islands, broadcasting mainly local news and weather content. Many hotels and bars in the more popular resorts also offer international sports satellite TV shown on wide screens.

Children

The Greek islands and their people welcome children warmly and there are very few places where they cannot be taken. Couples will often be cross-examined: do you have children? If not, why not?

Islanders regard children as an unmixed blessing, and crying babies or the fractious late-night behaviour of tired youngsters will be tolerated in village tavernas and cafés. Above all, life in the Greek islands is lived outdoors almost all year round and island youngsters are raised on a free-range basis, with the whole village and its surroundings as a playground. Visiting toddlers can easily join in.

Food

Food should not be a problem, even if your children are picky eaters who insist on a chips-only diet. These are on every island menu, as are other plain and familiar dishes such as fish and burgers.

Canned soft drinks are universally available, as are most well-known brands of sweets and chocolate bars, ice cream and ice lollies. Sticky cakes and sweet things from the *zakharoplasteion* (pastry shop) are also a hit with young children.

The seaside

The main attraction for families visiting the islands is the beach, and sea and sand are the focus of most family resorts. Greek seas have virtually no tide, so the sea is always at your doorstep and is usually calm enough even for young children to swim in safety. Sheltered, gently shelving, sandy beaches suitable for families with small children can be found on many islands.

Things to do

Children with an interest in wild flowers and wildlife will find the Greek islands a delight, with dozens of birds, lizards, tortoises, butterflies and other insects to identify and watch. Those with an interest in marine life will find the clear waters of inlets and harbours as full of sea creatures as any marine aquarium and will be fascinated by the varied haul unloaded by fishing boats each morning.

The end of any island pier always attracts a gaggle of junior anglers, and

Island children spend most of their time outdoors

simple hook-and-line kits are sold in all village shops.

Pedalos, canoes and other simple watersports equipment are for hire at all summer beach resorts and older children can use them with confidence in shallow waters and enclosed coves. Although island waters have very little tide, they do have strong inshore currents, so caution is advised. Bicycles for children and adults can also be rented at some resorts, and donkey-trekking into the hills is offered on several islands, including Amorgos, Corfu and Lesvos.

Children with an interest in history will find that ancient sites, medieval castles and deserted fortresses on almost every island offer a fascinating 'hands-on' lesson in the past, and younger children will enjoy scrambling

to the highest tiers of the ancient theatres.

In the unlikely event of poor weather, a visit to one of the many folk museums with their displays of costumes, kitchenware, tools, weapons and jewellery will help to keep children entertained.

Purpose-built facilities and entertainment for children are rarely provided in the Greek islands. Many villages have small playgrounds, though their old-fashioned wood and metal swings and roundabouts and rough gravel are potential hazards for smaller children.

Some larger resorts, hotels and apartment complexes have separate swimming pools for toddlers, and many package tour operators offer 'fun-clubs', childminding and babysitting services (*see* Practical Guide, *p179*).

Sport and leisure

The great sporting passions for Greeks – or, at least, younger Greek males – are football and basketball, which islanders play enthusiastically on dusty village pitches and watch avidly on television. Less energetic pastimes include billiards (most island villages have at least one café-bar with a billiard table) and backgammon or tavli, *which is universally played by older Greek men.*

Rowing, sailing and canoeing are increasingly popular, as is scuba diving. Greece offers an ideal climate for golf, but the islands are under-supplied with top-quality courses. Keen tennis players will find courts (sometimes floodlit) at major hotel complexes on Corfu, the Elounda area in Crete, Rhodes and Kos, but there are few public courts.

Golf

Although they offer an ideal climate for golf, there are only three 18-hole courses to be found in the Greek islands:

Crete Golf Club
Hersonnissos. Tel: (28970) 26000. www.crete-golf.gr

Corfu Golf Club
Livadi Ropa, 17km (11 miles) from Corfu Town. Tel: 26610 94220. www.corfugolfclub.com

Afandou Golf Course
Afandou, 19km (12 miles) from Rhodes Town. Tel: (22410) 51451. www.afandougolfcourse.com

Rock climbing

Climbing is one of the fastest-growing sports in Greece, and the island of Kalimnos, in the northern Dodecanese, has become a magnet for aficionados eager to test its excellent rock and to discover new routes. Climbing packages are offered by the **Hotel Elies** (*Tel: (22430) 47890. www.hotelelies.gr*).

Trekking and walking

The Greek islands are wonderful walking country, offering relatively gentle routes for a day's strolling or much more demanding itineraries lasting one or more days.

The Hellenic Alpine Club, which manages refuges in the Cretan mountains, publishes a range of guides and maps and offers useful advice.

Basic mountain safety rules must be obeyed even on shorter walks, especially in the mountains of Crete, as these and many other places are thinly populated and a sprained ankle far from help could spell disaster.

Greek Mountain Club of Hania
Tzanakakia 90, Hania, Crete.
Tel: (28210) 44647. www.eoshanion.gr

Dinghy and catamaran sailing

Small sailing dinghies and catamarans
for one to three people can be hired
by the day or the hour from many
island resorts. Nidri, on Lefkada,
is an excellent place to learn the
basics of sailing (*see p37*).

Flotilla sailing

For less confident sailors, flotillas, with
a lead yacht crewed by professionals,
are the ideal way to explore Greek
waters. A list of companies is available
from the Greek National Tourist Office
(*see p188*).

Scuba diving

Scuba diving is a fast-growing sport
in Greece, and there are now more
than 50 professional diving centres
throughout the islands. A list of
certified diving centres can be found
at *www.padi.com* or at the Hellenic
Professional Diving Association website
www.hellasdive.gr. Greek waters offer
excellent visibility, and there are
interesting dive sites, especially around
Crete, where the wrecks of vessels sunk
during World War II lie close inshore.

Waterskiing

Waterskiing facilities are available at all
holiday beaches in summer and there
are waterski schools at most major
resorts. For further information contact:

Greek Waterskiing Association
Aghios Kosmas, Athens. Tel: (210) 8947413.
www.waterski.gr

Windsurfing

Greek island waters, with their reliable
breezes, are perfect for windsurfing,
and boards are available for hire at
any sizeable resort. A number of
international events are held each year.

The west coast of Kos and the bay
of Nidri on Lefkada are rated among
the best windsurfing spots in the
Mediterranean.

Yacht charter

Steady winds, sunny weather and
thousands of anchorages make the
Aegean and Ionian Seas a delight for
sailors. You can sail at any time of year,
but April to October is the favoured
season. A full list of yacht charter
companies is available from the Greek
National Tourist Office (*see p188*).

Safe anchorage off the coast of Lefkada

Food and drink

The best island food is the simplest: fish straight from the boat, fruit and vegetables fresh from the field or orchard, served as salad with wild herbs and olives, or in stews and pies. Some dishes are ubiquitous, and most restaurants offer multilingual menus. Where they don't, you will be invited into the kitchen to choose from the simmer pots.

WHAT TO EAT

The choice of dishes may be narrower in smaller, less sophisticated island villages than in big and busy resorts, but the food is very often better off the beaten track. Look out, too, for places patronised by the islanders themselves and by Greek holidaymakers from the mainland – they are a more demanding clientele than most foreign tourists, and insist on quality, authentically Greek food.

Meals are rarely served course by course. *Meze* or *mezedes* are a culinary tradition that Greece shares with Turkey, the Middle East and North Africa, with a selection of small dishes served simultaneously.

Fish

For a fine fish dinner, Greeks go to a real *psarotaverna* (fish restaurant), which serves nothing but seafood. Fish is priced according to weight and category; you select your fish, which is then weighed and priced before gutting. Fish is always served with the bones in

and the head on (the cheeks and eyes are a delicacy). One sign of an authentic fish restaurant is a row of *oktapodi* (octopus) drying in the sun outside.

With demand for fresh seafood outstripping supply, many ingredients (especially octopus, *garides* (prawns) and *xifias* (swordfish)) now come from the freezer. By law, the menu must specify which dishes have been frozen.

Meat dishes

As with fish, so with meat: the best grilled meat dishes come from specialist *psistaria* (grill restaurants), which will serve an array of spit-cooked dishes – mainly chicken, lamb and pork – accompanied by chips and very little else. Most of the cuts will be familiar to visitors; more challenging authentic dishes include *kokoretsi* (a dish of lamb's liver and lights bound together with intestines and roasted). Greeks will often share a whole roasted sheep's head for a special treat.

Most non-specialist restaurants also serve a choice of oven-cooked meat dishes, collectively known as *mageirefta*, with favourites including *moussaka* (meat cooked in layers of bechamel sauce, cheese and aubergine), *giouvetsi* and *pastitsio* (veal stewed in a clay pot with different kinds of pasta); *stifado* (meat, usually pork, in a red wine and onion sauce); and *kleftiko* or 'robber's lamb', slow-roasted in paper or foil.

Vegetables and vegetarians
The traditional Greek salad known as *horiatiki* ('village salad') is a filling meal in itself, composed of tomatoes, onions, cucumber and olives, and usually topped with a slab of *feta* cheese. Dishes such as *gemista* (stuffed peppers or tomatoes) and *dolmades* may or may not contain meat, and many all-vegetable dishes such as *briam* (ratatouille), *fasolakia* (green beans stewed with tomatoes) or *papoutsakia* (aubergines roasted in oil with onion and tomato, called *imam bayildi* in Turkey) may be made with meat stock. The needs of vegetarians are not widely understood in Greece; if you tell the

waiter you are a *hortafagos* you will inevitably be offered an omelette or a salad, but you may also be offered fish or even chicken.

Island specialities
The tourist menu varies little from island to island, but a number of isles are known for their signature dishes and local products. Rabbit and pigeon are traditional dishes on Paros, Andros and Naxos; Kea is known for its smoked herrings, served as an accompaniment to a glass of local *retsina* wine. The traditional Cretan diet is rich in olive oil, wild greens, whole grains and pulses, and is credited with promoting the islanders' remarkably long average lifespan. Siros boasts about its unique San Mihali goat's cheese and an array of sweets including *loukoumia* ('Turkish' delight) and *halvathopites* (halva pies).

WHAT TO DRINK
Beer
Most beers served in Greece are strong lagers, brewed locally and served ice-cold. Imported beers and ales can be found in many resorts. Prices vary widely.

Imported and local spirits
Imported brands of whisky, brandy, vodka and gin cost a lot more than domestic spirits. Beware concoctions made with '*bomba*' – locally made raw alcohol used as a cocktail base and guaranteed to give you a crippling hangover. Greek brandy comes in

Strings of sun-dried tomatoes

three-, five- and seven-star quality. Best-known brands include Cambas, Samos and Metaxa raisin brandy, all of which are somewhat sweeter than most French brandies.

Greece's national spirit is *ouzo*, the clear, sweet aniseed-flavoured spirit which turns cloudy when water or ice are added. It is drunk at any hour of the day, often with meals, and the best brands come from Lesvos and Hios.

Raki and *tsipouro* (sometimes called *kourtimandia* in Crete) are potent, clear spirits made (like Italian *grappa*) from the skins and pulp left over after pressing grapes for wine. It is often drunk as a *digestif*, but you may also see early-rising market traders or fishermen enjoying a nip with the first coffee of the day.

Wines

Greek wine has improved enormously in recent years, and the islands produce a wide list of red, white and dessert wines at an equally wide range of prices: some of the most highly regarded cost as much as comparable fine French wines. At the everyday drinking end, whites are often better than reds. Some of the best island wines come from Kefalonia, Crete, Samos and Santorini, which is also famous for the sweet Vin Santo dessert wine. *Retsina* (resinated wine) is an acquired taste, but one worth acquiring quickly, as it is the most affordable of Greek wines. Many island tavernas also offer locally made wine '*apo to bareli*'

(from the barrel) and served in metal jugs; oddly, this is ordered not by the litre but by the kilo (half a kilo equals half a litre). Some of it is surprisingly good, some barely drinkable.

Soft drinks and water

With a few exceptions, tap water is drinkable on the islands but is often heavily chlorinated. Bottled water is available everywhere. All major soft-drink brands are available in shops, bars and restaurants everywhere. Freshly squeezed orange juice is also widely available in pricier cafés.

WHERE TO EAT

Below are restaurants listed on the bigger and more popular islands, as well as a handful of other places which stand out from the crowd.

The following table gives an indication of restaurant prices. The price rating indicates the cost of a three-course meal, per person, without wine.

Most island restaurants have a telephone, but only the more expensive and sophisticated eating places require reservations. Inflation has slowed, but prices may still increase by as much as 5 per cent from year to year, so only a rough price guide can be given.

Most restaurants in resort areas are open only from Easter until mid-October. Additionally, many restaurants in the most popular resorts are leased by the season – a restaurant may open in May, close in October and reopen the following year with a new name.

£	up to €30
££	€30–50
£££	€50–70
££££	more than €70

Ionian Islands
Corfu
Rex ££ Venerable Corfiot restaurant serving authentic Greek and Ionian cuisine.
Kapodistriou 66, Corfu Town. Tel: (26610) 39649. www.rexrestaurant.gr
Etrusco ££££ An eye-opening experience, Hector Botrini's restaurant shows what can be done with local ingredients.
Kato Korakiana village, Corfu. Tel: (26610) 93342.

Kefalonia
Vasso's ££ Traditional-style taverna serving oven-cooked dishes, grilled chicken, fish, salads and pasta.
Harbourfront, Fiskardo. Tel: (26740) 41276.
Tassia £££ The best restaurant in Fiskardo, with a menu that combines Greek, Italian and French influences.
Harbourfront, Fiskardo. Tel: (26740) 41205. www.tassia.gr

Lefkada
Sto Molo £ Very attractive *meze*-restaurant with cosy, prettily decorated dining rooms for cooler weather and, in summer, tables on the quayside.
Anatoliki Paralia, Golemi 12. Tel: (26450) 24879.

Paxos
Vasilis ££ The place to go for fresh fish and lobster in the cutest of Paxos's three harbour villages.
Longos harbour. Tel: (26620) 31587.

Argo-Saronic Islands
Kithira
Idragogeio £ The epitome of an island taverna, with a great choice of *mezedes* and good fresh fish.
Kapsali harbour. Tel: (27360) 31065). www.kithera.gr

Idra
Paradosiako ££
Delightful traditional *meze*-restaurant with blue wooden tables and chairs in a peaceful courtyard.
Harbourside, Idra. Tel: (22980) 54155.

Spetses
Tarsanas £££ Upmarket but friendly fish restaurant beside the old harbour. Crowded with Athenian visitors in summer, so book a table.
Palio Limani, Spetses Town. Tel: (22980) 74490.

Cyclades
Mikonos
Kiki's £££ A secret well kept by Mikonian cognoscenti, Kiki's serves island staples like grilled lamb and pork, but dresses them up with imaginative salads and trimmings.
Agios Sostis beach, Mikonos. No tel.

Santorini
Papagaios £–££ Bar-restaurant serving Tex-Mex and Greek grill cooking.
Main street, Oia. Tel: (22860) 71469.
Iliovasilema ££ This simple taverna with its wobbly tables by the sea is one of the best fish restaurants in the Aegean.
Ammoudi harbour, below Oia village. Tel: (22860) 71614.

Food and drink

1800 ££££ 1800 is the swankiest place to eat in Oia, with a sophisticated menu and an excellent wine list. Open evenings only.
Main street, Oia.
Tel: (22860) 71485.

Siros
Kouzina ££ Perfectly prepared Greek-Mediterranean dishes using only fresh seasonal produce.
Androu 5, Ermoupoli.
Tel: (22810) 89150.
www.kouzinasyros.gr

Tinos
Thalassaki ££
Imaginative menu based on local produce but with a flavourful modern twist.
Plataia Isternias, Tinos.
Tel: (22830) 31366.

Crete
Hania
Safran ££ Gorgeous modern Mediterranean restaurant in an old harbourside mansion.
Akti Tombazi 30, Hania.
Tel: (28210) 56333.

Dinos £££ On the inner harbour, this is a Hania favourite. Excellent seafood.
Akti Enoseos 3.
Tel: (28210) 41865.

Elounda
The Old Mill ££££
Excellent and expensive restaurant in one of the area's best hotels.
Elounda Mare Hotel, Elounda.
Tel: (28410) 41102.

Iraklio
Loukoulos £££ Long-established restaurant with good Italian cooking and pleasant ambience.
Korai 5, Iraklio.
Tel: (28102) 24435. www. loukoulos-restaurant.gr

Rethimno
Avli £££ Innovative restaurant (with luxury bedrooms available) with a Cretan-influenced menu and a superb wine list.
Xanthoudidou 22, Rethimno.
Tel: (28310) 58250.
www.avli.gr

Dodecanese
Kalimnos
Drossia £ Cheerful, affordable, with a menu featuring locally caught seafood. Harbourside location.
Limanaki Melitsacha, Massouri, Kalimnos.
Tel: (22430) 48745.
www.drosia-kalymnos.gr

Kos
Platanos £ Probably the best of an uninspiring choice of places to eat in Kos Town.
Plateia Platanou.
Tel: (22420) 28991.

Patmos
Benetos £££ Blends Mediterranean, Asian and Pacific Rim influences into an amazing culinary experience. Booking essential.
Sapsila, Patmos.
Tel: (22470) 33089.
www. benetosrestaurant. com

Rhodes
Alexis ££££ Magnificent seafood attracts celebrity guests. Worth a special trip.
Sokratous 18, Rhodes Old Town.
Tel: (22410) 29347.
www.alexis-restaurant. com

Mavrikos ££££ The best restaurant by far in Lindos, with a sophisticated and imaginative menu.
Kentriki Plateia, Lindos.
Tel: (22440) 31232.

Simi

Mylopetra ££££ An unexpected discovery on this tiny island, Mylopetra has one of the best wine cellars in Greece and a menu to match.
Simi town.
Tel: (22460) 72333.
www.mylopetra.com

Northeast Aegean Islands
Hios
Oinomageireion tou Iakobou £ Traditional-style taverna serving authentic Greek food and wine in the old part of Hios.
Kastro, Hora.
Tel: (22710) 23858.
Pirgos £££ Expensive but excellent restaurant, serving Greek and Middle Eastern-influenced food.
Enoseos 6, Hora.
Tel: (22710) 44740.
www.greciancastle.gr

Lesvos
Balouhanas £££ One of the best *ouzeri-mezedopoleions* in the islands, with a huge choice of seafood snacks to enjoy with a bottle of *ouzo*.
Iera, Perama, Lesvos.
Tel: (22510) 51948.

Limnos
O Glaros £££ A classic, simple quayside taverna serving superb fresh fish and lobster.
Limani, Mirina.
Tel: (22540) 22220.

Samos
Hippy's ££ This groovy beach bar and restaurant about 3km (2 miles) from the centre of Samos's second-biggest town is well named, with an amiably bohemian clientele.
Potami beach, Karlovassi.
Tel: (22730) 33796.
www.hippys.gr

Sporades and Evia
Alonissos
I Tsitsiria ££ The *psarosoupa* (fish stew) at this harbourside restaurant is memorable.
Patitiri harbour.
Tel: (24240) 65255.

Skiathos
Milos Taverna ££ Tables set on the pebbles beside the sea and a menu that serves traditional food and (surprisingly) some Chinese dishes.
Nea Paralia, Hora.
Tel: (24270) 21412.
Scuna £££ Overlooking the marina, but the service does not always match this restaurant's trendy aspirations. Go for the location (which is excellent) but not necessarily for the food, which sometimes disappoints.
Nea Paralia, Hora.
Tel: (24270) 22185.

Skopelos
Platanos £ Traditional taverna serving lavish helpings of grilled meat and authentic salads under the shade of a vast plane tree.
Plateia Platanos, Hora.
Tel: (24240) 23067.

Accommodation

Finding somewhere to stay is rarely a problem in the Greek islands in summer. There is accommodation to suit all pockets in all but the tiniest villages, where you may find the local shopkeeper is willing to rent a spare room (or, in summer, a camp bed in the garden or on the roof). However, almost all island pensions and hotels close between mid-October and April. You should also book well ahead for Easter and Koimisis (see p163) when thousands of expatriate Greeks return.

A twin room with en-suite costs from around €40–50 in a pension to €300 or more in a top hotel. The star ratings will give you an idea of the room rate for a double room for one night.

WHERE TO STAY

Price bands:

£ €50–100
££ €100–250
£££ €250–350
££££ more than €350

Ionian Islands
Corfu
Casa Lucia ££ Lovely self-catering cottages 3km (2 miles) from Gouvia.
Sgombou, Gouvia.
Tel: (26610) 91419.
www.casa-lucia-corfu.com
Corfu Palace ££££
Corfu's grandest and longest-established hotel.
Dimokratias 2, Corfu Town. Tel: (26610) 23926.
www.corfupalace.com

Kefalonia
Emelisse £££ The smartest (and most expensive) hotel on the island.
Emelissos beach, Fiskardo.
Tel: (26740) 41200.
www.arthotel.gr

Kithira
Hotel Margarita ££ Just outside the village centre, this 19th-century mansion has been turned into a boutique hotel.
Hora, Kithira.
Tel: (27360) 31711.
www.hotel-margarita.com

Zakinthos
Hotel Vanessa £ This small hotel boasts facilities that you would expect from somewhere much more expensive.
Kalamaki beach.
Tel: (26950) 26713.
www.hotelvanessa.gr
Castelli Hotel ££
Comfortable and affordably priced three-star hotel with modern facilities.
Agios Sostis, Laganas.
Tel: (26950) 52367.
www.castellihotel.com

Argo-Saronic Islands
Idra
Delfini £ The cheapest pension in Idra, near the dock.
Harbour, Idra Town.
Tel: (22980) 52082.
www.delfinihotel.gr
Bratsera ££ Delightful boutique hotel in the heart of Idra.

Hora. Tel: (22980) 53971.
www.bratserahotel.com

Spetses
Zoe's Club ££ Purpose-built complex of suites, studios and apartments.
Spetses Town.
Tel: (22980) 74447.
www.zoesclub.gr

Cyclades
Amorgos
Lakki Village ££ One- and two-bedroom family apartments.
Lakki, Ormos Aigialis.
Tel: (22850) 73253.
www.lakkivillage.com

Andros
Paradise Lifestyle Andros ££ Lovely mansion-hotel with sea views.
Outskirts of Hora.
Tel: (22820) 22187.
www.paradiseandros.gr

Folegandros
Anemomylos ££ An old windmill (*anemomylos*), which now houses the hotel's café-bar, stands on the edge of a 200m (670ft) cliff. It also has the island's only pool.
Hora. Tel: (22860) 41309.
www.anemomilos apartments.com

Mikonos
Semeli £££ A whitewashed enclave of charm and calm five minutes from the centre of Hora.
Rochari, Hora.
Tel: (22890) 27466.
www.semelihotel.gr
Theoxenia £££ Pop-Art-Deco hotel next to Mikonos's famous row of windmills.
84600 Kato Mili. Tel: (22890) 27466. www. mykonostheoxenia.com
Mykonos Blu ££££ The luxury Grecotel group's Mikonos flagship.
Psarrou, Mikonos.
Tel: (22890) 27900.
www.mykonosblu.com

Naxos
Chateau Zevgoli ££ This dinky hotel is a charming hideaway between the walls of a Venetian castle and the waterside.
Bourgos, Hora.
Tel: (22850) 26123. www. naxostownhotels.com

Paros
Yria Resort £££ Dazzling white bungalows near the beach, surrounded by bougainvillea, palms and jasmine.

Platasporas, Paros.
Tel: (22840) 24154.
www.yriahotel.gr

Santorini
Chromata £££ Rooms carved into the cliffside, in shades of turquoise, pink and gold.
Firostefani, Santorini.
Tel: (22860) 23227.
www.chromata-santorini.com
Zannos Melathron £££ Rooms and suites in a 19th-century wine merchant's mansion.
Pyrgos, Santorini.
Tel: (22860) 28220.
www.zannos.gr

Tinos
Voreades ££ Attractive, self-catering rooms 100m (110yds) from the ferry port.
N. Foskolou 7, Hora.
Tel: (22830) 23845.
www.voreades.gr

Crete
Hania
Metohi Kindelis ££ Super apartments in a manor surrounded by gardens and orchards.
Perivolia, Hania.
Tel: (28210) 41321.
www.metohi-kindelis.gr

Accommodation

Elounda
**Elounda Beach Hotel &
Villas £££** Two private
beaches, rooms, suites
and villas, and a spa
centre.
Elounda.
Tel: (28410) 63000.
www.eloundabeach.gr

Hersonissos
**Knossos Royal Villas
Aldemar Hotel &
Spa £££** This complex of
super villas has an
award-winning spa.
Limenas Hersonissou.
Tel: (28970) 27400.
www.aldemarhotels.com

Iraklio
Amirandes ££££ Opulent
and luxurious,
combining a collection
of split-level villas with
private pools and a
semi-private beach.
Iraklio 71110.
Tel: (28970) 41103.
www.amirandes.com
**Out of the Blue Capsis
Elite ££££** Fabulous,
luxury resort set on a
private peninsula about
20 minutes' drive from
central Iraklio. Superb,
Michelin-level Greek
food in seven different
restaurants.

*Agia Pelagia 75100,
Iraklio. Tel: (28108) 11112.
www.capsis.com*

Dodecanese
Kalimnos
Hotel Elies ££
Comfortable hotel
which also offers diving
and rock-climbing
packages.
Tel: (22430) 47890.
www.hotelelies.gr

Kastellorizo (Megisti)
Mediterraneo ££ Small
hotel with cool, airy
rooms and a bathing
ladder leading to clear
blue water just two steps
from your door.
*25 Martiou, Megisti.
Tel: (22460) 49007. www.
mediterraneo-megisti.com*

Leros
Archontikon Angelou ££
Six rooms and two suites
in a stylish pink-and-
white 19th-century villa
set in its own wooded
gardens.
*Alinda, Leros. Tel:
(22470) 22749; www.
hotel-angelou-leros.com*

Patmos
9 Muses £££ Small, serene
resort on secluded Sapsila

Bay, with four terraces of
bungalow suites.
*Sapsila, Patmos.
Tel: (22470) 34079.
www.9muses-gr.com*

Rhodes
Minos Pension £
Charming pension on
the highest point of the
Old Town, with cosy,
pretty rooms. Great
panoramic views from its
rooftop café-terrace and
from most of the rooms.
*Omirou 5, Rhodes Old
Town. Tel: (22410) 31813.
www.minospension.com*
**Avalon Boutique
Hotel £££** Six suites in a
16th-century building
above a cloistered
courtyard. All are prettily
furnished and decorated,
with en-suite bathrooms.
Best is the Thalassa, with
two bedrooms and a
living room on the top
two floors, and gorgeous
sea views from its private
terrace.
*Charitos 9, Rhodes Old
Town. Tel: (22410) 31438.
www.avalonrhodes.gr*
Melenos Lindos £££ The
Melenos Lindos has 12
gorgeous suites, each
with its own terrace.
Lindos, Rhodes.

Tel: (22440) 32222.
www.melenoslindos.com
Nikos Takis £££
Glamorous but affordable
boutique hotel.
Panetiou 26, Rhodes Old
Town. Tel: (22410) 70773.
www.nikostakishotel.com
**Amathus Beach Hotel
Elite Suites ££££** This
gorgeous annex to one of
Rhodes' best luxury
hotels offers the best of
all possible worlds. Suites
with private pools, direct
access to the beach, choice
of restaurants, fluffy
bathrobes and Bulgari
toiletries, spa treatments,
manicures and pedicures
set the tone, and the
service is immaculate.
The Old Town is a five-
minute taxi ride away (or
10 minutes by bus), but
you may find it hard to
tear yourself away.
Leoforos Iraklidou 100,
Ixia. Tel: (22410) 89900.
www.amathus-hotels.com

Simi
Les Catherinettes ££
Prettily decorated rooms
with harbour views in a
lovely old mansion.
Harani, Simi Town. Tel:
(22460) 71671. email:
julie-symi@ofenet.gr

Opera House ££ Set in
leafy gardens, not far
from the harbour.
Gialos, Simi.
Tel: (22460) 72034.
www.symioperahouse.gr

**Northeast Aegean
Islands**
Hios
Marko's £ With a dozen
simple rooms, this
guesthouse is marvellous
value.
Karfas village.
Tel: (22710) 31990.
www.marcos-place.gr

Ikaria
Cavos Bay ££ Unbeatable
location and excellent
value for money.
Armenistis, Ikaria.
Tel: (22750) 71381.
www.cavosbay.com.gr

Lesvos (Molivos)
The Olive Press ££ The
place to stay in the
island's prettiest village.
Yiali, Molivos.
Tel: (22530) 71205.
www.olivepress-hotel.com

Samos
Hotel Samos ££ Close to
the harbour with
comfortable rooms and
a rooftop pool.

Theo Sofoulis 11, Vathi.
Tel: (22730) 28377.
www.samoshotel.gr
Kerkis Bay Hotel ££
Friendly, family-run
hotel, in an unspoilt
harbour village.
Ormos Marathokambos.
Tel: (22730) 37202.
www.kerkis-bay.com

Sporades and Evia
Evia
Evia Hotel and Suites ££
New and stylish hotel
with very comfortable
rooms and fabulous sea
views from its poolside.
Only 90 minutes away
from Athens airport.
Marmari, Evia.
Tel: (22240) 31414.
www.eviahotel.com

Skiathos
Aegean Suites £££ A
stylish hotel on a
package-holiday island.
Ftelia, Skiathos.
Tel: (24270) 24066.
www.aegeansuites.com

Skiros
Nefeli ££ Modestly
comfortable and central
modern hotel.
Plagia, Skiros Town.
Tel: (22220) 91964.
www.skyros-nefeli.gr

Practical guide

Arriving

By air

International airports on Corfu, Crete (Iraklio and Hania), Karpathos, Kefalonia, Kithira, Kos, Lesvos, Mikonos, Rhodes, Samos, Santorini, Skiathos and Zakinthos handle charter flights from many European countries between April and late October. Charter flights for Lefkada land at Preveza, on the nearby mainland. Year-round scheduled services operate only to Athens and Thessaloniki on the mainland, with connecting flights to many islands including Hios, Ikaria, Limnos, Leros, Paros, Skiros, Naxos, Kalimnos, Kastellorizo and Kithira.

If you plan to fly within Greece, book your flights as far ahead as possible and reconfirm them (local travel agents on most islands can do this for you). On most islands, facilities at airports are basic and taxis are the only transport for passengers who are not on a package holiday. Car rental companies have desks at most island airports.

Real jet-setters can charter light aircraft or private helicopters to transfer them from Athens airport to smaller islands. Even the smallest isles have a helipad (used mainly for medical emergencies), as do a number of luxury resorts.

By sea

Many ferry companies ply the Greek island routes, connecting them with each other and with Pireas, the port of Athens. State-of-the-art Greek ferries dominate the Aegean Sea. Journey times range from under an hour for islands close to the mainland to around 14 hours (from Pireas to Rhodes). Ferries also operate from Thessaloniki, Kavala and Alexandroupoli on the northern mainland to the Sporades and Northeast Aegean islands, and from

On most islands, buses are timed to meet ferries

Igoumenitsa and Patra on the west coast to the Ionian isles. You can also arrive in Greece via Corfu with ferries from the Italian ports of Ancona, Bari, Otranto Venice and Brindisi; via Crete from Egypt and Israel; and via Rhodes, Kos, Samos, Hios and Lesvos from ports on the nearby Turkish coast. The *Thomas Cook European Timetable* has details of ferry times (*see also p185*).

Superfast Ferries (*www.superfast.com*) has the best services from Ancona and Bari in Italy to Corfu and the mainland ports of Igoumenitsa (opposite Corfu) and Patra (for onward connections to Kefalonia, Ithaki and Zakinthos). They have fast modern cruise-ferries with on-board facilities including restaurants, cinema, disco and swimming pool.

Passports and visas

Passports are required by all except European Union citizens, who may use national identity cards. British visitors need a full British passport and may stay indefinitely. Citizens of the USA, Canada, Australia and New Zealand may visit for up to three months without a visa, but citizens of South Africa do need a visa. Travellers who require visas should obtain them in their country of residence.

Camping

A list of island campsites is available from the **Panhellenic Camping Association** (*Mauromichali 9, 10680 Athens, tel: (210) 362 1560;*

www.panhellenic-camping-union.gr). Camping or sleeping rough on beaches is illegal, a rule which is widely ignored.

Children

There are few special facilities for babies or older children, except where provided for package-tour clients. Services often include babysitting for younger infants, playgroups for toddlers and activity groups for younger children. Baby milk, food and nappies are available at most mini-markets in tourist resorts and elsewhere from the *geniko emporio* (general store) or from pharmacies.

Climate

Each island has its own microclimate depending on the winds and sea currents. Generally, winters are mild and short, with rainfall at its highest and temperatures at their lowest in February, around 8–10°C (46–50°F), and much colder on the mountains of

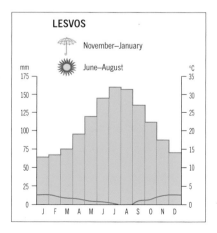

Practical guide

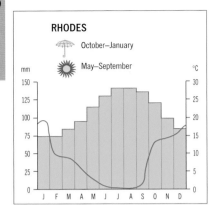

RHODES

October–January

May–September

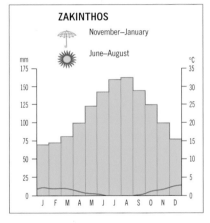

ZAKINTHOS

November–January

June–August

WEATHER CONVERSION CHART

25.4mm = 1 inch
$°F = 1.8 × °C + 32$

Crete and anywhere above 1,000m (3,280ft). By March, days are warmer, and April and May are changeable, with warm sunshine but a possibility of rain. It rarely rains between June and late September. Midsummer temperatures average more than 30°C (86°F).

Crime

The islands have relatively low rates of theft or violent crime against tourists. That said, normal caution should be exercised. Look after money, traveller's cheques, credit cards and other valuables.

Customs regulations

Normal EU rules apply. Non-EU visitors may bring in 200 cigarettes, 50 cigars or 250g of tobacco, one litre of spirits, two litres of wine or liqueurs, 50ml of perfume and 250ml of cologne. It is forbidden to export antiquities and works of art found in Greece.

Driving
Accidents

If possible, set up warning signs. Your hire car should be equipped with a warning triangle, but not all are. If someone is injured, the accident must be reported to the police (*see p182*). Passers-by in such cases are required to stop and assist. Contact the police as a precaution, even if the only damage is to vehicles.

If you can, write down the names and addresses of other drivers involved, the make and licence numbers of vehicles, the names of any witnesses and the date and time of the accident. If possible, take photographs.

Under no circumstances admit liability, sign any statement of responsibility, or lose your temper.

Breakdown

The **Automobile and Touring Club of Greece (ELPA)** provides tourist information and road assistance. *Tel: 10400* on all islands. ELPA's coverage of the islands is patchy, but there are competent vehicle repair shops and mechanics in most villages. **Express Service** (*tel: 154*) also provides a breakdown service on most islands.

Car hire

International chains are represented on all resort islands, with desks in island capitals and at international airports. There are also small local companies on almost every island, but car hire is less expensive if you hire through an international chain before leaving home. Rental cars, even from major chains, can be under-maintained. Check tyres, brakes, steering, spare tyre and lights before you leave the depot (*also see* Rules of the road, *below*). Full collision damage waiver (CDW), personal accident insurance, bail bond and liability cover are essential. Even international companies often exclude damage to the underside of the vehicle or the tyres from their CDW. Make sure your own insurance covers such damage.

Documentation

A full British or other EU driving licence is valid. Most other nationalities need an international driving licence.

Drink-driving

Penalties are severe and the best advice is to avoid alcohol when driving.

Fines

Police may impose fines for motoring offences on the spot but will not collect them there and then. The fine must be paid at a Public Treasury office or the traffic police station within ten days.

Fuel

Petrol costs around the European average. Lead-free fuel is widely available. It is forbidden to carry fuel in a container in the vehicle. Most petrol stations accept credit cards and most are self-service.

Navigation, maps and road signs

Romanised (conventional Western) spellings of Greek place names vary. However, the names are usually recognisable. On main roads, signs are in the Roman alphabet as well as in Greek. On some routes, there will be no signs.

CONVERSION TABLE

FROM	TO	MULTIPLY BY
Inches	Centimetres	2.54
Feet	Metres	0.3048
Yards	Metres	0.9144
Miles	Kilometres	1.6090
Acres	Hectares	0.4047
Gallons	Litres	4.5460
Ounces	Grams	28.35
Pounds	Grams	453.6
Pounds	Kilograms	0.4536
Tons	Tonnes	1.0160

To convert back, for example from centimetres to inches, divide by the number in the third column.

Rules of the road

Speed limits are 50kph (31mph) in built-up areas, 80kph (50mph) outside built-up areas and 120kph (75mph) on motorways. In practice, much lower speeds than these are advisable on poorly surfaced island roads.

Seat belts, where fitted, must be worn. You can be fined for not carrying a warning triangle, fire extinguisher and first-aid kit. Some rental cars lack these.

Electricity

Voltage is 220V AC. You may require an adaptor for the round two-pin sockets used in Greece. Power cuts are not uncommon, so take along candles and/or a torch. Appliances using US-style 110V power supply need a step-down transformer and socket adaptor.

Embassies and consulates

Australia

Dimitriou Soutsou 37, Athens.
Tel: (210) 8704000.
www.greece.embassy.gov.au.

Canada

Gennadhiou 4, Athens. Tel: (210) 7273400.

Ireland

Vassilissis Sofias 60, Athens.
Tel: (210) 7232771.
www.embassyofireland.gr

New Zealand (Consul General)

Kifissias 76. Tel: (210) 6924136.
www.nzembassy.com

United Kingdom

Ploutarchou 1, Athens.
Tel: (210) 7272600. www.fco.gov.uk

USA

Vassilissis Sofias 91, Athens.
Tel: (210) 7212951/9 & 7218401.
http://athens.usembassy.gov

Emergency telephone numbers

Ambulance *166*
General emergency *100* (manned by the police and dealing with crime, fire and medical emergencies)
Fire brigade *199* (cities and forests)
Coastguard *108*
SOS Doctors *1016*
Directory *11888*

Health

There are no mandatory vaccination requirements, but it is recommended that you have up-to-date immunisations against tetanus and polio, plus hepatitis A and typhoid if you intend to travel to some of the remoter areas. AIDS is present. Food and water are safe.

All EU countries have reciprocal arrangements for reclaiming the cost of medical services. UK residents should obtain the European Health Insurance Card from any UK post office. Claiming is laborious and covers only medical care, not secondary examinations (such as X-rays), emergency repatriation and so on. You are advised to take out adequate travel insurance, available through branches of Thomas Cook.

Measurements and sizes

Greece uses standard European metric measurements and sizes.

Media

The English-language newspapers *Athens News* (daily) and *Greek News* (weekly) give a quirky insight into national news and views. The bi-monthly glossy magazine *Odyssey* takes a more thoughtful approach.

British and European newspapers are on sale in most resort islands 24 to 48 hours after publication. The *International Herald Tribune*'s Greece edition includes a daily English-language edition of the leading Greek newspaper, *Kathimerini*. British news bulletins are broadcast on the ERT2 radio station (98kHz) at 2pm and 9pm.

The BBC World Service can be received on 9.41, 12.09 and 15.07MHz.

Money matters

The euro (€) is the unit of currency used in the islands. There are seven denominations of the euro note: €5, €10, €20, €50, €100, €200 and €500; eight denominations of coins: 1 cent, 2 cents, 5 cents, 10 cents, 20 cents, 50 cents and €1 and €2. Most major currencies and traveller's cheques can be exchanged at banks, post offices and travel agencies. The latter charge a higher commission but are open when banks and post offices are shut. Banks

Island roads, as here on Santorini, can be precipitous

and post offices generally open 8am–2pm weekdays only. Credit and debit cards are accepted in most hotels, shops and restaurants in most resorts. MasterCard and Visa are the most widely accepted.

National holidays

Note that dates for Easter and associated movable feasts, determined by the Greek Orthodox calendar, can vary from the Christian calendar by up to three weeks.

New Year's Day (1 January)
Epiphany (6 January)
Shrove Monday ('Clean Monday')
Independence Day (25 March)
Good Friday
Easter Sunday and Monday
Labour Day (1 May)
Day of the Holy Spirit (Whit Monday)
Assumption of the Virgin Mary (15 August)
Ochi Day (28 October)
Christmas Day (25 December)
St Stephen's Day (26 December)

Opening hours
Banks
See Money matters *on p183.*

Museums and sites

Opening hours given by official sources often bear no relation to the hours in force, which may change without notice. Most sites are open 8.30am–3pm, Tuesday to Sunday. Some major sites stay open until 7.30pm in summer.

Winter hours (November to March) are usually shorter.

Admission to most museums and archaeological sites under the aegis of the Ministry of Culture is free for university students and anyone under 19. There are reduced admission charges for EU citizens aged over 65. Admission is free for all on Sundays from November to March, on national holidays, on the first Sunday of each month except July, August and September, and on 6 March, 18 April, 18 May, 5 June and the last weekend in September.

Shops

These traditionally open from 9am–2pm and 6–9pm. Shops catering to tourists stay open longer. Most shops outside main resort areas close on Sunday.

Organised tours

Organised tours arranged by tour agencies at your resort can be an affordable way of exploring the island if you have no transport of your own or are reluctant to drive. Drawbacks include those of travelling with a group.

Pharmacies

A green or red cross marks the *farmakio*. Greek chemists have some medical training and can advise and prescribe medicines for common ailments. Pharmacies open during normal shop hours from Monday to Friday.

Places of worship

Sunday services at most Orthodox churches are held from around 7.30am and last for some hours. Decently dressed visitors (which means long trousers and shirt sleeves for men, below-the-knee and arm-covering dresses for women) may attend. There are Roman Catholic churches on Tinos, Siros and Corfu.

Police

See Emergency numbers on *p182*.

Postal services

Most larger island villages have a post office, distinguished by its prominent circular yellow sign. They are normally open weekdays during shop hours, but city-centre post offices are also open on Saturday mornings. It is often quicker to change money at a post office than at a bank. Stamps (*grammatosima*) are also sold at kiosks and postcard shops. Parcels for posting must be inspected by the post office clerk before sealing. Air-mail letters take three to six days to reach the rest of Europe, five to eight days for North America and slightly longer for Australasia. Postcards take much longer.

Public transport
Island buses

Buses are the only public transport available on the Greek islands. Frequencies and services are usually geared to the needs of islanders, not of tourists: buses are cheap, but do not always serve the sights you want to go to at the time you want to go, if at all, though some islands, notably Rhodes and Skiathos, have excellent services adapted to the needs of visitors. Crete has a good long-distance bus network. Double-check the destination with the conductor: destination boards often indicate where the bus has come from, not where it is bound. Buy tickets on board.

Ferries

Pireas, the port of Athens, is the main gateway to the Aegean islands. Many nearby islands are served by hydrofoils, some of which go from Zea Marina, about 3km (2 miles) away. Hydrofoils and ferries also go to Evia, the Cyclades and the Northeast Aegean islands from Rafina, about 30km (19 miles) east of Athens. Other mainland ports with ferries to the islands include Rafina and Laurio, near Athens (for the Cyclades); Patras (Ionian Islands); Githio (Kithira and Crete); Volos (Sporades); Kavala (Thassos) and Alexandroupoli (NE Aegean). Schedules change monthly. For up-to-date timetables and online booking with most ferry lines, see *www.gtp.gr*

Taxis

Taxis are everyday transport for islanders and will go virtually anywhere. Fares are metered and most taxi drivers are friendly, honest and helpful, though overcharging is

Language

THE GREEK ALPHABET

Greek	Name	Pronounced
Α α	alpha	a
Β β	beta	b
Γ γ	gamma	g, but becomes y in front of e and i
Δ δ	delta	d
Ε ε	epsilon	e as in 'extra'
Ζ ζ	zeta	z
Η η	eta	e as in 'eat'
Θ θ	theta	th
Ι ι	iota	i
Κ κ	kappa	k
Λ λ	lamda	l
Μ μ	mi	m
Ν ν	ni	n
Ξ ξ	xi	x
Ο ο	omicron	o
Π π	pi	p
Ρ ρ	rho	r
Σ σ	sigma	s
Τ τ	taf	t
Υ υ	ypsilon	u
Φ φ	phi	ph
Χ χ	chi	ch as in 'loch'
Ψ ψ	psi	ps
Ω ω	omega	long o

NUMBERS

1 ena
2 dio
3 tria
4 tessera
5 pente
6 exi
7 epta
8 okto
9 ennea
10 deka

USEFUL WORDS AND PHRASES

yes/no	neh/okhee
please/thank you	parakahlo/efkhareesto
hello/goodbye	yasoo/andeeo
good morning/good afternoon/evening	kahleemehra/ kahleespehra
goodnight	kahleeneekhtah
OK	endacksee
excuse me/sorry	signomee
Help!	voylthia!
today/tomorrow	simehra/ahvrio
yesterday	ektes
open/closed	anikton/kliston
right/left	thexia/aristera
How much is it?	Poso kani?
Where is a bank/ post office?	Poo ine i trapeza?/ to tahithromeeo?
Where is the bus station?	Poo ine o stathmos ton iperastikon leoforeeon?
stamp	grammatoseemo
doctor/hospital	yahtros/nosokomeeo
police	assteenomeea
I would like...	Tha ithela...
menu	menoo
toilets	tooahlehtess
mineral water	emfialomeno nero
bread	psomee
salt/pepper	alahti/piperi
fish/meat	psaree/kreas
beer/wine	beera/krasee
Cheers!	Steen eeyeea soo!/yahmas!
coffee (with milk)	kafes (me gala)
Can we have the bill, please?	Mas fernete ton logariasmo, parakalo?
I don't understand/ Do you speak English?	Then katalaveno/ Milate Anglika?

common when going to and from airports. Beware, too, in Athens and Pireas, where taxi drivers are notoriously dishonest with foreign tourists.

Senior citizens

Older visitors accustomed to cooler climes may find the islands pleasanter in April or May, or after mid-September, when temperatures are less scorching. Just as Greeks love children, they respect older people, but age brings no privileges. Older people are expected to fend for themselves; for example, when boarding a bus or ferry. In a country where queuing is almost unknown, this can be trying.

Smoking

Officially, smoking in indoor public places has been banned since 2009, and the younger generation of Greeks is much less likely to smoke tobacco than their parents. This said, many Greeks are still enthusiastic smokers, and the ban does not apply to outdoor cafés and restaurants. Many upmarket hotels have 'cigar bars' where visiting oligarchs can enjoy fine Cuban smokes, and the shisha waterpipe has made a comeback with younger Greeks. There are shisha cafés in Rhodes, Kos, Mikonos, Santorini and on many other islands.

Sustainable tourism

Thomas Cook is a strong advocate of ethical and fairly traded tourism and believes that the travel experience should be as good for the places visited as it is for the people who visit them. That's why we firmly support The Travel Foundation, a charity that develops solutions to help improve and protect holiday destinations, their environment, traditions and culture. To find out what you can do to make a positive difference to the places you travel to and the people who live there, please visit *www.makeholidaysgreener.org.uk*

Telephones

There are public phone booths in most towns and large villages. These accept coins, credit and debit cards, and pre-paid phone cards. Mobile phone coverage extends to all the islands. Roaming charges within the EU are capped, so mobile phone users from other EU countries should pay no more for voice calls than they would at home. However, heavy extra charges may apply for text messages, email and web use. Mobile phone users on islands close to the Turkish coast should be aware that their phone may automatically connect to a Turkish network, and so incur much more expensive charges.

Time

GMT+2 hours (+3 hours in summer). Clocks change in spring and autumn on the same date as other EU countries, but this does not always coincide with non-EU countries.

Tipping

Service is included in restaurants and it is common also to leave small change on the table. This also applies to bars and cafés. There is no pressure to tip in hotels, but it is always welcomed. In taxis, 'keep the change' is usual.

Toilets

Standards vary enormously, but there have been dramatic improvements. Toilets in cafés and tavernas are usually better than public facilities. Greek plumbing is easily blocked, so except in modern hotels do not flush toilet paper but put it in the bin provided.

Tourist information

The Greek National Tourist Office (GNTO) provides a range of information which includes hotel listings and details of sites and events. *GNTO Head Office: Tsocha 7, 11521 Athens. Tel: (210) 870 7000. www.visitgreece.gr*

Outside the Greek islands
Australia and New Zealand
37–49 Pitt Street, Sydney, NSW 2000. Tel: (09) 241 1663.
United Kingdom and Ireland
4 Conduit Street, London W1R 0DJ. Tel: (020) 7495 9300.
USA
305 East 47th Street, New York, NY10017. Tel: (212) 4215777.

In the Greek islands
Corfu
Corfu Tourist Office, Alykes Potamou, 491 00 Corfu. Tel: (26610) 37520.

Crete
Hania Information Office, Kriari 40, 731 00 Hania. Tel: (28210) 92943. Iraklio Tourist Office, Papa Aleksandrou E 16, 712 02 Iraklio. Tel: (2810) 301830. Rethimno Tourist Office, Eleftheriou Venizelou, Ktirio Labyrinthos, 741 00 Rethimno. Tel: (28310) 29148.
Kefalonia
Information Office of Argostoli, Provlita Teloniou (Customs Office Dock), 281 00 Kefalonia. Tel: (26710) 22248.
Lesvos
North Aegean Tourist Office, Tz Aristarchou 6, 811 00 Mitilini. Tel: (22510) 42512.
Rhodes
Prefecture of the Dodecanese, Plateia Eleftherias 1, 851 00 Rhodes. Tel: (22413) 60515.
Samos
Samos Information Office, 25th Martiou 4, Vathi, 831 00 Samos. Tel: (22730) 28582.
Siros
Ermoupoli Information Office, Thimaton Spercheiou 11, Ermoupoli 841 00 Siros. Tel: (22810) 86725.

Travellers with disabilities

Facilities for travellers with disabilities in the Greek islands are poor but are gradually improving. Wheelchair ramps are rare. Pavements are usually narrow and uneven, and roads often deeply potholed. Most island sites are atop steep hills. Before leaving the UK, contact **RADAR** (*www.radar.org.uk*) for general help and advice.

Index

Acknowledgements

Thomas Cook Publishing wishes to thank the photographers, picture libraries and other organisations, to whom the copyright belongs, for the photographs in this book.

AA PHOTO LIBRARY 22, 90, 94, 95, 96, 97, 101, 103, 106, 109, 133, 152, 165 (Steve Day); 82, 132 (P Enticknap); 17, 58, 60, 62, 64, 69, 78, 169, 178 (Terry Harris); 136, 147, 151 (R Moore); 19, 85, 148 (Ken Patterson); 23, 43, 49, 117, 121, 124, 127, 129, 131 (A Sattin); 51, 55 (P Wilson); 26, 27, 45, 46, 53, 54 (James Tims)
TREVOR DOUBLE 8, 13
DREAMSTIME.COM 1 (Freesurf69), 11 (Marianna Raszkowska), 119 (Madmacs), 161 (Yiannos1), 167 (Assimina Antonakopoulou), 183 (Tomas Marek)
ROBIN GAULDIE 7, 20, 104, 105, 112, 113
TERRY HARRIS 29, 66, 71, 73, 75, 98, 145
PICTURES COLOUR LIBRARY 34, 39, 143, 159
SPECTRUM COLOUR LIBRARY 15, 138
THOMAS COOK 36, 68, 89, 111, 157
JAMES WATT 155
WORLD PICTURES/PHOTOSHOT 123

For CAMBRIDGE PUBLISHING MANAGEMENT LIMITED:
Project editor: Karen Beaulah
Typesetter: Paul Queripel
Proofreaders: Penny Isaac & Jan McCann
Indexer: Marie Lorimer

SEND YOUR THOUGHTS TO
BOOKS@THOMASCOOK.COM

We're committed to providing the very best up-to-date information in our travel guides and constantly strive to make them as useful as they can be. You can help us to improve future editions by letting us have your feedback. If you've made a wonderful discovery on your travels that we don't already feature, if you'd like to inform us about recent changes to anything that we do include, or if you simply want to let us know your thoughts about this guidebook and how we can make it even better – we'd love to hear from you.

Send us ideas, discoveries and recommendations today and then look out for your valuable input in the next edition of this title.

Emails to the above address, or letters to the traveller guides Series Editor, Thomas Cook Publishing, PO Box 227, Coningsby Road, Peterborough PE3 8SB, UK.

Please don't forget to let us know which title your feedback refers to!